THE
DUCHOVNY
FILES

THE
DUCHOVNY
FILES

THE TRUTH
IS IN HERE

PAUL MITCHELL

ECW PRESS

CANADIAN CATALOGUING IN PUBLICATION DATA

Mitchell, Paul
The Duchovny Files: the truth is in here

ISBN 1-55022-284-8

1. Duchovny, David. 2. Television actors and
actresses — United States — Biography.
3. X-files (Television program).   I. Title.

PN1992.4.D83M57 1996   791.45'028'092   C96-990054-6

Many thanks to Jenifer Linville, Scott Mitchell, Paul Challen,
Jennifer Trainor, Paul Davies, and Bob Pipe.

Design and imaging by ECW Type & Art, Oakville, Ontario.
Printed by Kromar Printing, Winnipeg, Manitoba.

Distributed in Canada by General Distribution Services,
30 Lesmill Road, Don Mills, Ontario M3B 2T6.

Distributed in the United States by Login Publishers Consortium,
1436 West Randolph Street, Chicago, Illinois, U.S.A. 60607.

Published by ECW PRESS,
2120 Queen Street East, Suite 200,
Toronto, Ontario M4E 1E2.

TABLE OF CONTENTS

DAVID
DUCHOVNY
BIOGRAPHY

HUNGRY FOR LOVE

On a certain night in 1991, in the Largo Pub in Los Angeles, a young man named David Duchovny got up before a small audience to read his poetry. He was a remarkably handsome young man, elegantly tall and with a brooding face that suddenly became light and open when he smiled.

If some of the people in the audience recognized him — not for being a writer but as an actor — that would not have been unusual in L.A. At poetry readings in this celebrity town it is not uncommon to discover that famous actors and directors have a secret hankering for the "pure" and "simple" artistic life of the poet. At this time David Duchovny was hardly famous, but he had gained some notoriety during a three-episode guest starring role on the second season of *Twin Peaks*, that strange and groundbreaking show that had already begun to lose its way, not to mention its audience. On the other hand, perhaps the audience wouldn't have recognized Duchovny, who had appeared on the show as a transvestite police officer — in wig, make-up, and padded bra.

But Duchovny had not worked since the *Twin Peaks* shoot had ended and he felt a strong need to stand in front of an audience. While he had been writing poetry for years — for his first artistic impulse had been to write — this was his first public reading. Being a reflective and rather self-absorbed person, he had at least some unconscious understanding of his own need to be loved and admired by strangers. So he got up that night and read a poem that he had written for a woman friend, about thresholds and being afraid of never belonging.

Duchovny was thirty-one years old; he had taken up acting relatively late, at the age of twenty-six, and had not been in California for long. But the signs were good that he might have a successful career ahead of him and he had to admit to himself that the idea of becoming a movie star was pretty attractive. Still, he hadn't given up the idea of writing, which after all was much closer to the life of the mind that he had lived as a graduate student in English literature. Indeed, he felt some conflict between what might be called the mind and the body, between intellectual work and the instinctive, physical existence of the actor. It was a conflict that would only deepen with time.

Duchovny read his poetry and as the audience clapped he came down again. If this was just a small dose of attention from strangers, then what he would receive in just three or four years was a veritable avalanche. But how could David Duchovny have predicted the future? How could he have predicted that he would soon find himself swimming in love, drowning in admiration? And that rather than help him to know himself it would cause even greater alienation?

Mind you, fame would have its rewards as well.

WELCOME TO SECOND AVENUE

The Lower East Side in Manhattan has never been a desirable address — unless, of course, you have ambitions to sell pickles or *shmattes* (which is Yiddish for rags but really means clothing) or even to be a Torah scribe. Back in the seventies and eighties it was also a good place to be a heroin addict — lots of supply available. In the nineteenth and early twentieth century it was the tenement-filled quarters of the Jewish immigrants who had fled Eastern Europe for a better life.

In later years the Jews had mostly moved to nicer neighborhoods uptown or in the Bronx and newer waves of immigrants — Puerto Ricans, Chinese — came to take their place.

The Lower East Side is, however, an interesting place to grow up and from which to observe the extraordinary range of human hunger, aggression, and sheer hunger for survival. As Duchovny would later say, after growing up in the Lower East Side it was almost impossible for him to be shocked by anything. David William Duchovny was born on August 7, 1960 (under the astrological sign of Leo, for those who care), and taken from the hospital by his parents to view the world from their apartment at Eleventh Street and Second Avenue, diagonally across the road from the Second Avenue Deli. His father claimed that the name "David" came from the famous statue by Michelangelo that stands in the Uffizi museum in Florence. No doubt Duchovny's women fans would agree that the actor is as beautiful as the marble statue, and in truth he does share something of the deep, slightly wounded look that Michelangelo miraculously put into the statue's eyes. Duchovny, however, refers to the name in a more typical self-deprecating way, using it to make fun of his so-called understated acting style. "A statue," he says. "And I've tried to pattern my acting style on that as well."

That Duchovny's parents continued to live in the northern section of the Lower East Side showed not only that they were definitely not rich, but also that they held a certain loyalty to the neighborhood. David's father, Amram Ducovny, was born in Brooklyn of Russian Jewish parents. The family name, Duchovny (Amram dropped the silent 'h'), means spiritual in Russian, a meaning which appealed to David's imagination. After graduating from New York University, Amram spent some time as a journalist in Europe and the Middle East before becoming a publicist for a cultural organization, the American Jewish Committee. Amram was also a writer of sorts, producing a number of books that were mostly compilations of quotations by famous people. Their titles — *The Wisdom of Spiro T. Agnew, David Ben-Gurion in His Own Words, I Want to Make One Thing Perfectly Clear* (this last one on Richard Nixon) expressed a liberal outlook, a dislike of Republicans, and support for the state of Israel. Another of his books, exposing frauds against old people, showed his interest in advancing the social good.

David has a strong resemblance to his father, especially the prominent nose and lips. From his father he inherited a strong sense of irony — a form of humor and an unromantic way of looking at the world that is shared by many Jews. When as a kid David would complain that if only it wasn't raining out he could play outside, his father would answer, "If my grandmother had wheels she'd be a trolley," an admittedly puzzling response to a young boy. David also likely received his interest in sports and music from his father; Amram followed baseball and was a Billie Holiday fan.

By the time David was making his name as Fox Mulder in *The X-Files* his father had left the United States for France, where he had taken to sitting in cafés and trying to write a novel. There is no question that David's mother has been the greater influence on him and that it was she who raised the children after she and Amram divorced. In interviews David speaks much more about her, he still visits her in the old apartment, and his undergraduate thesis at Princeton was dedicated to his mother and his siblings — though not to Amram. But tellingly, David's own early ambitions combined those of both his parents. Like his mother, who is a school teacher, he wanted to become a university instructor and impart knowledge to students (or at least to make a steady living doing so). And like his father, he wanted to be a writer. It is tempting to speculate that by combining their interests David was unconsciously trying to bring his mother and father back together, to metaphorically "undo" the divorce that had so devastated his childhood.

TOO BUSY THINKING

David's mother, Meg (short for Margaret), was born and raised in Scotland, far from the Brooklyn of his father's experience. David described their union as the Highlands meets Coney Island. Her philosophy of life was stoic rather than ironic and she believed that hard work and dedication were how you made a life. From her, David received his strength of will and his determination to succeed. Whenever young David complained to *her*, about having a runny nose or some minor pain, she would say in her Scottish accent that it was better than "a stine a hinda loog" — which translates as "a stone behind the ear." In other words, don't complain — it could be worse.

An early experience of Meg's was David's closest encounter with an unexplained phenomenon. Back in

Scotland when she was a girl, Meg had once seen her grandfather come into the house and peek into the crib of her younger brother. The only problem was that her grandfather had been dead for some time, the victim of a drowning.

Until the divorce, Meg was a stay-at-home mother. Then, needing to raise three children, she went to work as a teacher, eventually becoming head of the lower school of Grace School Church in Manhattan, a Catholic school, where she still was as David was becoming famous.

It was this unlikely mix of Russian Jewish and Scottish genes that produced David. And what was the result of this clash of cultures? "You get kind of that Protestant work ethic combined with Jewish guilt and introspection," David has said. "So you get someone [who wants to] go out and do a lot of stuff and change the world, but he's too busy being depressed and sitting and thinking about it."

You also get someone who has ambitions but at the same time deep reservations about those ambitions. Someone who has pursued success but who feels that choice is illusory and that he is not really in control of his destiny but a prisoner of it. Someone who in any case feels that the success is unearned and therefore not real or deserved.

Someone who is not at peace with himself.

OUT AT BVORSCH

When the baby David was brought home to Second Avenue he was no doubt greeted with a mixture of excess enthusiasm and suspicion by his four-year-old brother, Danny. Danny would grow up to direct television commercials in Los Angeles and even to work on one of his younger brother's projects, *The Red Shoe Diaries*. But like most older siblings, he sometimes gave his younger brother a rough time. He nicknamed him "Ugly," "Big Nose," and "Big Lips." He told his friends that his brother, who was unusually quiet, was retarded. None of this had any scarring effect, however, and David would grow up to name Danny as the person he most trusted.

Six years after David's birth came his sister Laurie. Like her mother, she would become a teacher (most recently at St. Anne's in Brooklyn) and continue to live in New York. "The biggest softy" is how she described David after his rise to fame.

Across from the apartment house was the St. Mark's graveyard, one of the old cemeteries in New York in which were buried early Dutch inhabitants of the island. David tells the story of how the neighborhood kids would use the graveyard as a baseball diamond and the flat gravestones as bases. Instead of shouting using the regular names such as first base or home, the kids would use the names on the stones, calling out "Safe at Bvorsch" or "Out at Steiveson!" True or not, the story gives a sample of the sly humor that his friends and fellow actors would come to know well.

As a kid David loved archaeology and especially dinosaurs, and had a set of plastic figures which he would play with in the bathtub. This elaborate imagining was the reason, or so his father believed, that at the age of six he announced that he wanted to grow up to be a bathtub. (To this day Amram phones up his

son and says, "So, still a failure, huh?") Outside of the
family he was shy and preferred not to say much.
Slightly chubby, with a round face and his hair even
then falling over one eye, he was an attractive child.
But he was self-conscious about that large nose, saying
that his face was "at war with itself." The shyness
would continue through adolescence.

David's very first acting experience came in the fifth
grade, when he played one of the Three Magi at Grace
Church in Manhattan. (He was an early example of a
mixed religious upbringing.) But the role had less of
an impact on him than seeing his father's own play, *The
Trial of Lee Harvey Oswald*, performed off-Broadway for
a brief run in November 1967. Written by Amram and
Leon Friedman, the play posed the question of what
would have happened if Oswald had not been killed
by Jack Ruby and so had stood trial for the murder of
John F. Kennedy. The stage of the Anta Theater on West
52nd Street was transformed into a courtroom and
the audience acted as jury as they listened to argu-
ments from the prosecution, the defence, and Oswald
himself, all based on actual evidence and testimony. In
all likelihood the shortness of its run had something
to do with the less than glowing review from Clive
Barnes, the influential critic of the *New York Times*. Not
only did Barnes think the use of this material was
exploitive and morally questionable given the gravity
of the subject matter (the assassination of a president),
but he thought the device of the trial was unoriginal
and the material presented already too well-known.
Young David, however, was not concerned with any
of that. Instead, he was fascinated by the way an actor
sat on the stage for the entire first act. David turned

to his father and asked how the man could stay there without needing to go to the bathroom.

THE TRAUMA

Introspective by nature, David needed the security of his family. But when he was eleven his parents divorced, an emotionally traumatic experience for the child that he has never fully recovered from and that, by his own admission, continues to guide his emotional life even as an adult. "I don't think you ever recover from something like that," he has said. "You are forced into an adult world of emotions that you aren't prepared to deal with." While his parents tried to explain that sometimes the love between a husband and wife doesn't last, he was too young to emotionally or intellectually separate himself from the event; he was afraid that his parents would withdraw their love from him. "So it can define the way you deal with love for the rest of your life," he once ruminated.

Worse, he thought that somehow he was responsible for his father's leaving. (It is common for children to transfer the blame onto themselves and to look for a more easily understandable explanation.) About the time of the separation his father once said to David, "Will you stop that infernal whistling?" Afterwards he felt sure that it was his whistling that had driven his father away.

His mother was now forced into the workforce, taking her away from home during the day to teach in an elementary school. If anything she pushed the children even harder to do well academically, in order to ensure their future stability. David would come to believe that the divorce was at the center of the emotions driving him to succeed in university and beyond. But most significantly of all, for David Duchovny the person *and* the actor, it taught him to hold back or bury his emotions beneath a calm exterior.

"I think it caused me to repress a lot because I was supposed to be like, the hero in the family and do well in high school and do well in sports," he said, analyzing himself. He did not want to, or perhaps he didn't feel that others wanted him to, express all that he really felt. Perhaps if he had he would have screamed and wept and broken things and swung out his fists — all the things that actors get praised and paid for but which embarrasses almost everyone in real life. Elsewhere he has said that "It became a technique of survival not to feel things too deeply," but a person who doesn't allow himself to feel also doesn't fully connect with life and with others, doesn't commit himself to relationships or experience. And Duchovny has admitted that the memory of the divorce has made it hard for him to fully commit himself to a relationship that would lead to marriage. Even when he was involved in a long-term romance with actress Perrey Reeves he would say that for this same reason marriage was not in their future.

As a result of this repression some people find Duchovny, despite his sense of humour and his charisma, to be somewhat distant and emotionally reserved. They think, perhaps, that he is a bit cold. But a person cannot really prevent himself from feeling emotions. He can submerge them, sometimes so deeply as to lose awareness of their presence, but they remain like some inner wound that never heals. What has attracted casting directors to Duchovny is not merely his good looks or even his acting ability, but a sense of this deep pain that he draws upon for his acting technique even as he suppresses it.

After the divorce, David's mother Meg altered the spelling of the name she kept, returning the silent 'h' to Duchovny. As the children grew older the way they chose to spell it became a sign of loyalty to one parent or another. Daniel, the eldest, who had known his father the best, retained Amram's spelling. Laurie, the youngest, wavered back and forth, spelling it sometimes with the 'h' and sometimes without. In support of his mother, David decided to spell his name ever after as Duchovny. There was no doubt that he was his mother's son.

THE BURDEN OF VIRGINITY

Meg urged her children to study hard and apply themselves to the job of excelling at school, which is just what David did. He must have made her proud when he won an academic scholarship to Collegiate School, a prestigious and elite Manhattan prep school for boys. (Another student during David's time there was John F. Kennedy Jr.) Along with studying hard at Collegiate, David played baseball and basketball and excelled. He was given a nickname — Duke — and found himself in a different world from the Lower East Side he knew, a world where children grew up in penthouse apartments facing Central Park and had

everything they desired. One day a friend invited
David over and he was amazed when the elevator
opened not onto the apartment hallway but directly
into the friend's apartment.

At Collegiate Duchovny became friends with
another student named Jason Beghe. They were soon
best friends, a relationship that continues happily to
this day, but they could not have known that it would
result in David becoming an extraordinarily successful
and wildly popular television star. In fact, it was Beghe
who first caught the acting bug. Back then, however,
they spent their time hanging around and trying to
scare Duchovny's little sister Laurie by putting stockings over their heads and chasing her around while
they waved spatulas and egg beaters.

As for girls, Duchovny was more of a wallflower. As
a teenager he went on few dates. That big nose of
his (the rest of him eventually caught up, more or
less) and his share of acne didn't help his self-esteem.
He grew his hair long and parted it on the side, a
seventies look he now considers hideous. Perhaps his
awkwardness came in part from his mother's constant
encouragement to work hard and succeed at school,
giving him little time to imagine himself as anything
other than a good student. Later, discovering an interest in acting, he would find himself attracted precisely
because actors could let go of that self-control, could
scream or cry, expressing the most extreme emotions.
But for now he relaxed by himself, smoking mari-
juana and listening to his record albums, saving his
money for a long time to buy the triple live album
Yessongs. (The old records are still in his mother's
apartment.) And he continued to play baseball and

especially basketball. (Though he reached the height of six feet, it wasn't enough to slam-dunk the ball.)

Despite the shyness, Duchovny lost his virginity at a surprisingly — even a shockingly young age. Fourteen. A friend of his had had sex with a girl when he was only twelve and kept taunting Duchovny about it, who saw it more as a burden relieved when the event finally occurred.

For his senior yearbook at Collegiate, Duchovny chose two quotes, the authors of whom revealed his mixture of all-American athleticism and intellectual precocity. One was by Joe DiMaggio, the great New York Yankee. The other was by John Berryman, the great American poet who took his own life.

TWO

HIGHER LEARNING

While he was still in prep school, Duchovny decided that he wanted to become a writer. But he felt that he lacked the courage to simply try to write and survive on menial jobs; no doubt his mother's urging to succeed academically didn't help. "I didn't grow up with much money and my mother instilled in me [that] the gutter is only a few feet away," he would say later. "I just wanted to put a few more feet between me and the gutter." So he decided to get a higher degree, become a university professor, and write in his spare time.

Duchovny's marks at Collegiate School as well as his ability on the basketball court earned him a place at Princeton University. With a beautiful campus on over 2,000 acres in Princeton, New Jersey, Princeton is one of the country's most prestigious universities with a high reputation for its liberal arts courses. It is also known as one of the capitals of the rich and casual preppy style — buttoned-down shirts and dock shoes. "I discovered what preppy really was," Duchovny once joked, "a level of Biff-dom I'd never seen before."

At Princeton Duchovny majored in English literature and proved himself a good student who concentrated on his studies rather than using college as an opportunity to engage in one long party. Later he would feel some regret for foregoing the "wild and crazy" experience that seems an American rite of passage. While he played baseball as well as holding a spot on Princeton's basketball team during his sophomore year, university-level competition eventually proved too tough for him.

In December of his first year he saw a young woman student and immediately fell for her, even joining a politics class because she was in it. Eventually she succumbed to his charms and the two remained an item for four years. While he has not mentioned her name in interviews, it seems a good guess that she is the Bonnie to whom his undergraduate thesis is dedicated to along with his mother and siblings. Duchovny has mused that if they had met later in life they probably would have married. She was his first long-term relationship and the lesson that he seemed to have learned from it was to be wary of getting into another. Being with her, he has said, taught him not to lie and cheat in a relationship — sins that he sheepishly admitted to having committed. It should be noted, however, that Duchovny has a tendency to dramatize his romantic relationships and sex life for the press and to make it sound exciting and risky. On the other hand, he is likely telling the truth.

THE MIND/BODY PROBLEM

To fulfil his undergraduate degree at Princeton, Duchovny wrote a thesis which he submitted in March 1982. *The Schizophrenic Critique of Pure Reason in Beckett's Early Novels* is a substantial work of more than 150 pages, a dense and fascinating thesis that shows its author to be well-versed in literary technique. Duchovny alludes frequently not only to Freud but also to Kafka, Dante, Nietzsche, Marx, Shakespeare, etc., as well as such gods of postmodernism and deconstruction as Jacques Lacan and Michel Foucault. Worth noting is the absence of many references to previous critical books on Beckett; Duchovny was clearly an ambitious student who wanted to set out his own ideas rather than rehash the thoughts of others.

And yet while Duchovny proved himself capable of talking the talk, he also felt free enough (and gutsy enough) to use an almost offhand, colloquial writing style. His wonderfully arrogant opening sentence dismisses all the critics who have come before him, and who he can't be bothered to quote: "Beckett is misunderstood." This is deliberately provocative stuff, intended to raise the eyebrows of his professors.

While Duchovny's reasoning in the thesis is exciting and original, it is also somewhat cavalier. He makes assertions without backing them up sufficiently and as often as not offers bravado rather than argument. At the same time, while the work is written with vigor, a reader can feel that it has been accomplished with more doggedness than pleasure. And even the greatest David Duchovny fan must admit that it is no real treat to read, particularly for the non-specialist.

Duchovny's ideas about the Irish-born author are not of primary concern here. What is of concern is what might be divined of Duchovny's own personality by a reading of his thesis. And while it might be a stretch to apply Duchovny's own words about Beckett to himself, nevertheless it is a fascinating and revealing exercise. Duchovny begins his thesis with a quotation from one of Sigmund Freud's case histories, and it is to Freud who the young scholar most frequently calls upon, if not always with approval. Freud, of course, is the great originator of the theory of human personality based on repression. Indeed, according to Freud, civilization itself is possible only by the repression of the darker human instincts and emotions. Memories, traumas, and significant emotions are all repressed by people with sometimes damaging effect; it is the job of psychoanalysis, Freud's invention, to uncover these repressions through such techniques as hypnosis and dream analysis.

Duchovny had been learning to repress his own most significant emotions since the age of eleven when his parents ended their marriage. It is hardly surprising that this would make for a person who is less than happy under the surface of his appearance, or that it would have a negative effect on his ability to make lasting and committed relationships. Duchovny never underwent psychoanalysis or some other therapy (at least there is no record of it) but he would eventually do something that would serve the same purpose: he would become an actor. Only when acting could he feel free to express deeper emotions and to act out the sort of hidden desires that cannot be risked in real life. As Duchovny himself has said, an actor can sleep with whichever woman or even man he wants, can commit murder, and suffers no consequences. For Duchovny acting would become a substitute for therapy, a way of uncovering deep emotions and impulses in a safe manner.

In his thesis on Beckett, Duchovny saw in the author's fictional characters a version of his own dilemma which would, paradoxically, fully manifest itself only after he became an actor. His mother had urged him to pursue the life of the mind and Duchovny had worked hard to sharpen his analytical technique, his critical faculties. But there was another part of him, the emotional part, which desperately wanted to emerge. This emotional part of one's being is allied with the body rather than the mind and expresses itself through the body — by weeping, raging, laughing, through violence and through sexual passion. It was the body that Duchovny had learned to repress and that was in conflict with his mind.

According to Duchovny the student, the characters in Samuel Beckett's novels suffered from a similar condition, a kind of separating of the human per-sonality into the two areas of intellect and emotion, of mind and body. The character of Murphy in the novel named for him, Duchovny wrote, "replicates his conflicting desires for mind, body, or oblivion into separate selves like an amoeba self-dividing." Later in the thesis Duchovny wrote tellingly of "a world of disunified parts where mind and body watch each other like hesitant strangers." Was the devoted student only writing of Beckett, or was he revealing, perhaps unconsciously, his own dilemma? Did he too feel divided, as if his own intellect and emotions were strangers to one another?

YALE

Duchovny did well enough at Princeton to win a Mellon Fellowship to Yale University. Set in New Haven, Connecticut, Yale was over two hundred and fifty years old and one of the finest universities in the country. It attracted some of the best students in the U.S. who were drawn by the reputation of its faculty of intellectual stars, including Harold Bloom, John Hollander, Jay Hillis Miller, and Geoffrey Hartman, some of whom became Duchovny's professors. Later their influence could be felt in Duchovny's precocious and allusive conversation; for example, when he talked to one interviewer about God treating Moses badly (proving that life is simply unfair) he was showing the influence of Harold Bloom.

At Yale Duchovny had to earn his master's degree before starting work on his Ph.D. Like most graduate students, in his second year he became a teaching assistant and was permitted to teach undergraduates, the first instructing experience on the way to becoming a professor. To qualify for the M.A. he had to sit for a slate of oral examinations during which professors ask questions to ascertain the breadth and depth of a student's knowledge of literature. The orals are every graduate student's nightmare. To prepare, Duchovny studied for nine hours a day until his head felt so heavy he thought it would tumble from his shoulders.

But pass he did, moving on to his Ph.D. and completing the necessary course work before beginning to work on his dissertation. A dissertation is a major effort in which a student is expected to make an original contribution to literary criticism. It can take years of research and writing and reach 400 pages in length, and if a student is very fortunate he will eventually turn it into his first published book. (Publishing is essential to success in the academic world.) Some dissertations take on the narrowest of subjects, finding some little unexamined corner in the work of an author. But Duchovny was nothing if not ambitious and the title he came up with was to say the least impressive: *Magic and Technology in Contemporary American Fiction and Poetry*. The idea he wished to investigate went beyond literature to the subject of ethics. Technology, Duchovny believed, was a kind of amoral knowledge, neither good nor bad but merely factual. The workings of the atomic bomb was an example. If people had the knowledge and technology to build a bomb then they *would*, regardless of whether it was good for humanity or not. Magic, on the other hand, was something else. It was a "primitive technology" used by tribal peoples and earlier societies in place of the strictly scientific technology of modern society. Magic was not amoral at all, but had a system of moral codes built into its belief system. For example, there was black (bad) magic and white (good) magic.

Duchovny's thesis was that certain American writers such as Norman Mailer, Thomas Pynchon, James Merrill, and Ishmael Reed, had tried to give modern technology the moral properties of magic. They wanted to "infuse" technology with a moral code. His dissertation would examine this attempt. His suspicion was, however, that the writers were doomed to failure, for it was impossible to bring morality to technology. Modern society was like Faust selling his soul to the devil. The temptation was just too great. If technology can build a more powerful bomb then it will, regardless of the consequences. People simply did not have the willpower to resist.

Nor did Duchovny. In just a few years he would make his own Faust-like pact, winning fame, beautiful women, and wealth. And like Faust, he would feel sometimes as if he had traded in his soul.

During his second year at Yale, Duchovny began making friends with students at the Yale Drama School. He had begun to have doubts about becoming a teacher, a profession he had pursued out of a desire for stability rather than out of love. The academic world seemed too protected and unreal to him, cut off from real life. The drama students seemed to be having a lot more fun than he was and he preferred hanging around with them than with other English majors. However, he wasn't thinking about acting but about writing plays and screenplays and he managed to talk his way into a playwrighting class. Later he

would not be able to remember the full title of the
first play he wrote, only that it began *The Last Free*
Advice of and ended with the name of the character. "It
was kind of funny and tragic, like me," he recalled.

THREE

TOSSING PRETZELS

Jason Beghe, Duchovny's best friend from Collegiate School, had decided to become an actor when he was 25. He went to New York City, began studying with a teacher, and in 1985 landed his first film role in *Compromising Positions*. Since then he has appeared in *Thelma and Louise* and other films and has done guest spots on *Melrose Place*, *Picket Fences*, *NYPD Blue*, and other television shows.

His ideas about acting would prove to be very different from his friend Duchovny's, less intense and more balanced. "As an actor you not only give the audience something that you've put a lot of time into but also

share a part of yourself with them. If it's a good role
you also discover something about yourself in the
process. I don't know what could be more exciting."

But Beghe himself was just beginning when he convinced Duchovny to audition for some television commercials. He thought there was something about his
friend that would appeal to the camera. Certainly the
awkward young boy who considered himself an ugly
duckling had grown into the beautiful swan. He was
six feet tall, with thick brown hair and a lock falling
over his eyes like some mischievous Tom Sawyer. Moody
hazel eyes with an actual twinkle in them. A mole
on his right cheek. His body was handsomely well
proportioned and modestly muscular without being
pumped up like some cartoon action hero. His voice
wasn't strong, he even sounded at times as if he had
marbles in his mouth, but there was something seductive and intimate about it. But perhaps what made him
most appealing was not his good looks but that quiet
brooding quality, the sense that there was some hurt
visible in the eyes and the turn of the mouth.

Duchovny didn't get the first commercials that he
tried out for but got the nod from the casting director
of a commercial for Löwenbrau beer. On the set (a
noisy bar) Duchovny found himself not just nervous
but terrified, yet he managed to do what he was told,
which was to throw a pretzel in the air and catch it in
his mouth. For this feat of dexterity he was paid
$9,000, twice his yearly salary for teaching at Yale.
His mother had told him that hard work would pay
off, but she hadn't told him anything about earning
fast money by throwing pretzels and looking nice for
the camera.

Fast money aside, Duchovny was not going to be foolish about this bit of luck. He continued to study and work at Yale, even if his desire for the academic life slipped away even more. The commercial work led to some auditions for television pilots and during the Christmas break he flew to Los Angeles to test for three shows. A limousine picked him up at the airport and deposited him at the Sunset Marquis, a first-class hotel. The tests took longer than expected and he had to phone the Yale office — from poolside at the hotel — to tell them he was sick and would miss teaching his first classes.

He didn't get the roles. Duchovny was still a neo-phyte actor and his style, wrongly characterized as understated, left directors wondering if he was doing anything at all up there. Well, it seemed a good thing he still had a lecture room to return to.

That was, until he was unexpectedly cast in a new film by Henry Jaglom. It was 1987, and although the film wouldn't be released until two years later it pushed Duchovny into taking an active decision in determining the future that he wanted, or thought he did. He quit Yale, abandoned his thesis, and embarked on the actors' life.

THE ART OF SELF-INDULGENCE

Henry Jaglom is one of those rarest of creatures in American film-making, a successful independent director who has never sold himself to a Hollywood studio or compromised the vision of his art. He has

his loyal fans and his detractors (there are some people who would rather have root canal work than sit
through a Henry Jaglom film) although it is also true
that the mass movie-going public has largely ignored
him. His real popularity is on the art-house circuit, in
urban centers such as New York, and at film festivals
around the world.

Jaglom is often compared to Woody Allen, and
while the comparison is superficial it is not without
some truth. Jaglom too cares largely about the relations
between men and women and his films are extremely
talky as his characters discuss their inability to find
lasting partnerships, their sexual frustrations, their
quirky human traits, and their infidelities. But while a
Woody Allen film seduces the audience with humor
and melancholy romance and is always exquisitely
made, Jaglom's films (like those of the late John
Cassavetes) are deliberately rough and improvisa-
tional in style. He draws out his actors — often
well-knowns such as Karen Black and Orson Welles,
who are willing to work cheap — to use their own
real lives in creating their characters so that the films
have almost a documentary quality to them. As a result
they are by turns fascinating, dull, revealing, irritating, self-indulgent, profound, and superficial.

The concept of *New Year's Day* was typical Jaglom,
combining a clever premise with lots of improvisa-
tional possibilities with practicality. Jaglom himself
(an unattractive man and an amusing but annoying
presence in many of his films) would play a writer who
is returning to New York from a stay in Los Angeles
after separating from his wife. (In real life Jaglom
and his wife had indeed split up.) He expects to find

his apartment empty — he had sublet it during his absence — but discovers that the women who have been staying there are holding a New Year's Day party before leaving. During the course of the film guests would arrive and depart, people would talk about changing their lives, relationships would move forward or break off. The film could be shot entirely in a single location (the apartment), making it inexpensive to produce.

As in his previous films, Jaglom did not wish to use a fixed script. Instead, he would rely heavily on the actors' spontaneity as the camera rolled, encouraging them to open up, to let out their emotions, to be honest and even confessive. This method actually suited Duchovny at this very early stage of his acting career for two reasons. The one he gave was that he wasn't yet comfortable taking words on a script and making them seem like his own. The one he didn't give was that he could actually draw on his real self, turning the role into not just an implicit but almost an explicit form of therapy.

In the film Duchovny plays Billy, the former boyfriend of a woman at the party (Lucy, played by Maggie Jakobson) who is moving to California. He shows up at the apartment to win her back and she reluctantly invites him to stay for the party. Duchovny as Billy is dressed in a leather jacket, jeans, and running shoes, and he looks very young. Having cheated on Lucy before, he can't stop himself from hitting on two women at the party, eventually falling into bed with Lucy's messed-up roommate (who afterwards tries to kill herself). Lucy throws him naked out of the apartment.

Rumors have circulated that Duchovny's role was created by him largely from his own life and it is interesting to recall his comments about having to learn the hard way about not cheating in a relationship. There is an extraordinarily revealing scene in the film in which Jaglom's character, Drew, sits down with Billy and proceeds to ask him questions — in effect, to analyze his Casanova personality. If Duchovny used acting as a kind of substitute therapy, a way of liberating his emotions, then this scene is a paradigm of that process. Drew asks him, "So what is this bullshit about?" He recognizes in Billy a version of himself, but whereas he at least can truly relate to people, he believes that "Underneath your bullshit there seems to be more bullshit." Billy replies that he can't get rid of the lying because he thinks it is more interesting than his real self, and also that he is afraid to show his real self because it is "corrupt in some way" and "dark." But because women don't see his real self, his darkness, he mistreats them for misunderstanding him — "I punish them." He admits that he loves talking about himself, that he feels compelled to kiss women who are nice to him, and that he has a compulsion to seduce even men, only "without the kiss." When Drew asks if all of this started with his mother, Billy says yes, that his mother is overprotective and still overly involved in his life. "I'm not able to make the transition from being an adolescent or someone who's sheltered by his mother," he says, and the result is "fucking up" his relations with women. His mother is the one woman who sees his darkness and who likes it, taking it for profundity.

Listening to this conversation between an old and a

young hustler is like eavesdropping on a real conversation. The viewer can feel Duchovny's young, seductive quality, his self-absorption, and also the compelling intensity of his dark and confused feelings.

Later Duchovny would say that he saw both advantages and disadvantages to Jaglom's improvisory approach, but that while he recognized the film was not to everyone's taste he was not ashamed of his first work either. The popular critic Leonard Maltin called it both illuminating and pretentious, which is true enough, but it is also one of Jaglom's best films to date, with appealing performances from all the actors and without the pointless meandering of some of his earlier work.

THE METHOD

New Year's Day would not be released until 1989 (it is not unusual for low-budget films to have long post-production periods) and it was not the sort of film to make Duchovny either rich or a star. But the experience of making it was enough for him to realize that he wanted to be an actor and just might have the talent for it. He quit Yale (against his mother's wishes) and moved back to New York, beginning a period of more than a year that would be one of the most difficult of his life. It was difficult because the work did not come. "I was going from one endeavor considered by the people who do it as the deepest intellectual and most spiritual endeavor you can do — to spend your life with books," Duchovny would say, "to something where the parts might be superficial and I might not be any good at it. So I had a lot of shame about the fact that I wanted it."

Duchovny's agent told him not to tell casting directors that he was a Princeton and Yale grad as they would likely be intimidated by him, even if the degrees did constitute "a worthless pedigree" in Duchovny's opinion. (As far as he could tell, there was no correlation between the intelligent people he met and the schools they attended.) In fact, Duchovny found it a little hard to believe that his years of hard work in the academy now counted for zip. He was starting from scratch all over again. Nevertheless, his ambition wasn't small. He wasn't thinking of theater or television but movies. And he wanted to be a star.

While his family did not approve of this sudden and apparently crazy career change, Duchovny's brother Daniel would be able to understand it better in retrospect. David, he realized, was always the good son, the one who was expected to do well at school and achieve academic status. But this pressure was emotionally repressive to him and it isn't surprising that he would want to break away and make his own life — one in which the emotions rather than the intellect, in which fantasy rather than rationality, came first.

Duchovny knew that he had a lot to learn about acting, especially since he had been holding back his emotions rather than expressing them since he was a child. So he decided to study like his friend Jason Beghe, signing on with an acting teacher named Marsha Haufrecht who was associated with the famous Actors' Studio in New York.

Founded in 1947 by Elia Kazan and others, the Actor's Studio is based on the Stanislavsky method developed by a famous Russian director. It was simplified, however, and made more emotionally charged in its translation into the American style known as method acting. (Henry Jaglom studied at the Actors' Studio in the 1950s.) Perhaps the most famous among the many well-known actors to emerge from the Studio was Marlon Brando, a much more expressively emotional performer than Duchovny but one he greatly admired.

Haufrecht taught Duchovny that the basis of acting is truth. He had to trust what he was feeling at any given moment in a scene, even if the emotion didn't seem the called-for response. For example, if he felt like giggling at a funeral then he should giggle. If instead he acted solemn he might please the director but his performance would be a lie.

Duchovny worked at opening himself up emotionally so that he could scream, yell, or cry. He had been working for years at heightening his analytical powers, only to discover that being too self-aware and analytical can be paralysing for an actor or at best lead to a boring delivery. Instead, he had to trust his emotions and his instincts. Even so, his "understated" acting style was there from the beginning. Duchovny himself believes that this style has its roots in his academic life: "I probably got it from Yale — this horrible, all-levelling relativism" he says of a style that tends to flatten out responses to high emotion. Just as likely, though, is that it can be traced to the emotional repression that began with his parent's divorce when he was eleven and his attempt not to feel things too deeply. Duchovny's understated style is in fact a style of emotional repression; it is not that nothing is happening, but that it is happening underneath the surface, visible only in Duchovny's eyes, in subtle gestures, in the inflection of his voice.

Later on *The X-Files*, Duchovny would use a method-acting approach to enter into the character of Fox Mulder. One of the techniques of method acting is to find an event from one's past or an emotional feeling and draw on it to understand the motivations of the character being played. Duchovny would say, "Mulder and I are different cats. But I do have some personal beliefs that I think can be easily substituted. I'm someone who believes in powers that are greater than the physical, but I don't necessarily give them form."

Although his goal wasn't to appear on the stage, Duchovny did begin to get roles in off-Broadway productions even while he was at Yale. Two plays he performed in were *The Copulation Machine of Venice, California* and *The Green Cockatoo*. The latter was by Arthur Schnitzler, the turn-of-the-century Viennese playwright who shocked contemporary audiences with his frank depictions of sexuality and his uncovering of erotic dalliances beneath the polite facade of bourgeois society. (Freud considered Schnitzler to be his artistic double, revealing in art the same secrets he was discovering through psychoanalysis.) The play was a foreshadowing of the kind of offbeat films with strong sexual themes that he would be cast in before winning the role of Fox Mulder.

Considering that Duchovny wanted to act in movies, it was strange that he admitted to enjoying the experience of theater more than film. "There's something different about working with an audience," he said. "Because you're working *with* an audience. You're making an experience together in the present moment, rather than making something for future or recorded use." While he would be tense in the first moments of a play, he found himself quickly relaxing into the part. Performing live, Duchovny said, felt like "bliss." In contrast, filming was a nerve-racking experience. He constantly felt high levels of anxiety and tension. Nevertheless, it was film that he wanted to pursue, not theater. And in America, if an actor wants to be a movie star, there is only one place for him to go.

Hollywood.

FOUR

THE HEISENBERG PRINCIPLE

Jason Beghe and Duchovny both needed to make a living while they were auditioning for (and not getting) acting parts, and so they enrolled in bartending school. They took the deluxe two-week course rather than one-week and Duchovny would joke that his mother hung up his bartending diploma alongside the ones from Princeton and Yale. The two friends got a job at a bar called the Continental on 13th Street in New York. But the place had little business and then they would spend the night drinking Dom Perignon champagne. According to Beghe's fuzzy memory of the period, they were both finally fired.

Later, in one of his attempts at becoming David Duchovny the author, he worked on a novel that was based on this time. Called *Wherever There Are Two*, after Jesus' saying that wherever two people are gathered is a church, it was about a man like himself who worked as a bartender at the Continental. Written in a highly self-conscious third-person style, it contained plenty of drugs and sex somewhat in the manner of Jay McInerney's *Bright Lights, Big City* and Bret Easton Ellis' *Less Than Zero*. Although it wasn't successful (he believes that unlike his quiet acting style, he tends to overwrite, drowning out the story with too much detail), Duchovny thought it had some good writing in it. He particularly remembered one surreal chapter called "The Spider and the Fly" in which the main character dreamed that whenever he pulled down his fly to urinate a spider would come out.

Among Duchovny's other writing projects was adapting a short story by the American writer Charles Bukowski for the stage. Most of the time, however, he concentrated on poetry which he would sometimes read in public. Among the influences on his work were John Ashberry, whom he admired for being both concrete and elusive at the same time, John Berryman for his earthy, sexual quality, and the high modernist Wallace Stevens. He also liked to read about science and claimed, as others have in this century, that science was really a kind of poetry. He has, for example, been fascinated by the Heisenberg uncertainty principle which states, in effect, that it is impossible to observe something without changing it. No doubt the Heisenberg principle would take on greater poignancy for Duchovny after *The X-Files* made him famous and, becoming the object observed, he felt that being watched by fans and hounded by journalists was changing *him*.

After the start of *The X-Files*, Duchovny would have little time for writing of any kind, although he would try to scribble down a poem whenever he could — in a restaurant at lunch or in an airplane. He would continue to think about a couple of writing ideas that had been simmering for a long time, but he had to admit that he found himself afraid to actually tackle them. What if it turned out that he wasn't the writer he thought he could be? Even so, he continued to hold writing as an important future goal and claimed that it came to him "more naturally than anything else besides playing with a ball." What he was also saying by implication was that acting did not come naturally to him at all. On the contrary, for him being emotional in front of a camera was difficult and painful work.

Moving to Los Angeles in order to be near the Hollywood film industry did not put an immediate end to Duchovny's dry spell. He worked for a catering company, wrote a couple of magazine articles. After success finally came he would say that he spent that hard time leeching off his friends.

When *The X-Files* began and Duchovny had to live in Vancouver for ten months of the year he would miss Los Angeles and believe that it had become his home. But coming back during the hiatus he would find that it really didn't feel like home after all and that he no longer had roots or a sense of place anywhere. The realization came to him that whichever place he had lived in last was the one that most felt like home. Quoting Proust he would say with resignation, "The only true paradise is paradise lost."

He did manage to get a small part as a friend at a birthday party in the Mike Nichols' directed comedy *Working Girl* starring Harrison Ford and Melanie Griffith. But another small role did not come until 1990's *Bad Influence*, a film which briefly resuscitated the career of Rob Lowe after his erotic home-movie making became a public scandal. (Perhaps Duchovny was thinking of Lowe when he mused in an interview about how fame circumscribes a person's life, making public what is rightfully private.) But not until Duchovny earned a guest spot on a cult television show did he have a breakthrough, if a modest one.

THE FEMININE SIDE

David Lynch's weird dramatic series, *Twin Peaks*, was a surprising hit during its first season in 1989–90. FBI Special Agent Dale Cooper (played by Kyle Mac-Lachlan) was sent to a small town in Washington to investigate the murder of a teenager named Laura Palmer. The murder investigation and the strange characters populating the show kept the audience tuned in, but in the second season (during which the ratings faltered) a new story line was needed. So Agent Cooper was framed for stealing drugs and another agent sent to investigate. Cooper was supposed to have worked with this other agent, Dennis Bryson, on a previous case and respected him. He did not expect Bryson — played by none other than David Duchovny — to arrive in Twin Peaks dressed in full drag.

It was casting director Johanna Ray who had a hunch that Duchovny could pull off the role of transvestite Dennis/Denise. Duchovny himself was thrilled to get the three-episode role, even if it would be a strange acting experience. He figured that there was no reason to worry about his reputation in the industry considering that he really didn't have one. At the same time he couldn't help wondering whether this would be the start *and* finish of his career. Perhaps he should have recalled how a similar role in the movie *The World According to Garp* launched the career of John Lithgow.

But Duchovny only had a day and a half to prepare for the role and hardly knew how to go about it, even if he did like to think that he was in touch with his feminine side. Most of the time was spent making him look like a woman. He spent hours in a trailer in the San Fernando Valley where the show was shot, first applying Nair to his legs to remove the hair. It came off like dog hair and made him feel nauseous to look at it, but he thought he had nice legs and joked that his sister Laurie was jealous of them. When he pulled on the panty-hose — very slowly — he found that it made his gut hang over the top so that he felt ugly rather than womanly. The bra, which was an under-wire and padded, hurt when he put it on. The costume people had given him "big tits" as he put it, "like a loaf of bread . . . the kind that go straight across without any differentiation. Kind of like Mrs. Doubtfire." He found that the bra hurt. The dress had a high neck so that at least he didn't have to shave his chest. A wig gave him rich hair down to his shoulders and bangs. The clip-on earrings he wore had been borrowed from a friend. Later Duchovny, who liked to make sexually provocative statements to interviewers, would say of dressing like a woman, "I liked it more than I can say, and it disturbs me still," but in fact it was more painful than anything else and gave him a new appreciation of what women endure to look good for men.

Duchovny's performance as Dennis/Denise is low-key but amusing and shows off his comic talent. He speaks in more or less his normal voice, if a touch softer, but he moves much more than usual. His head seems to wave and float on his shoulders. The episodes were aired in December 1990 and January 1991. In the first he gets to catch a bouquet thrown by a bride at a wedding. "I had an unfair advantage. How many of those girls were varsity wide receivers?" In the second episode he expresses interest in a woman, surprising Agent Cooper who expected him to be gay. "I may be wearing a dress," Dennis/Denise said, "but I still put my panties on one leg at a time, if you know what I mean."

Duchovny had some personal concerns before the airing of the episodes. He worried about what his parents would think, and to make matters worse his father had to undergo a heart bypass operation. After seeing the show, his mother on the phone responded by saying, "You look thin. Are you eating enough?" As for his father, when Duchovny went to visit him in the hospital, Amram let all the nurses know that his son just played a transvestite.

Twin Peaks was cancelled at the end of the season, but it had made some people take notice of David Duchovny. The dry spell was over.

Quickly Duchovny found himself getting what he really wanted — film roles. He had a minor part, but more than a bit, in the 1991 adolescent comedy *Don't Tell Mom the Babysitter's Dead*, a successful film that wasn't as bad as the title suggests. More remarkably he won two leading roles in films released in that same year. They both had one thing in common: sex.

Julia Has Two Lovers was a low-budget romance directed by Bashar Shbib. It was co-written by Shbib and Daphna Kastner, who also starred as a children's writer unhappy in her relationship with a boorish man named Jack who, despite his desire to marry her, seems not to feel much passion. Then she receives a phone call from Daniel, played by David Duchovny. Again he looks remarkably young. When the audience first sees Daniel he is in his underwear, pacing an empty apartment. He sings "Happy Birthday" to her, pretending that he meant to phone someone else, and the result is a conversation that lasts the entire day. They tell each other about early sexual experiences and other intimacies as they cook, shower, clean house. The dialogue is hesitant and not slick and is clearly being improvised in part. Duchovny as Daniel is very funny. After Julia tells him that she is blond and beautiful (in fact she's dark and only modestly pretty), he tells her, "I'm also tall, blond, curvaceous, with big breasts." At one point he tapes the phone to his head to leave his hands free.

The next day Daniel comes to Julia's beachfront house for lunch and they have romantic sex. But after he leaves she discovers that he has used the same trick on other women. Daniel admits that he does it because he's afraid of becoming close to someone, to showing his real self. But he loves Julia and has a ridiculous argument with Jack over her. In the end Julia tells him to call her in a month and we see her alone, dancing on the beach.

The film was shot with a very small crew and the script, like Henry Jaglom's, had little structure or formality. (Kastner would later appear in a Jaglom film, *Eating*.) The sound quality is imperfect and it has an almost amateurish look. Yet it is a pleasing, funny, and even romantic film, and Duchovny is both intense and comic. For Duchovny it was a fun film to make, even if he had no personal interest in erotic phone conversations, calling himself more a "visual" person. Interestingly, the character that he played, like Duchovny himself, had trouble revealing his true self to others and making a commitment to a woman. While the film did not get wide play in the theaters or a great deal of attention, it did receive some positive reviews and eventual video release. Bruce Williamson, the regular film critic for *Playboy*, was impressed by this first encounter with Duchovny, calling him a "handsome actor from the same gene pool that brought us Alec Baldwin and Richard Gere." Leonard Maltin called it "cheaply made, unevenly acted, but the premise is solid enough to keep you engrossed till the end."

Far more memorable — and more controversial — was *The Rapture*. Written by Michael Tolkin, a highly accomplished screenwriter and novelist (his novel *The Player* was the basis for the acclaimed Robert Altman film of the same name), it was also his directorial debut. Its budget, while closer to Hollywood stand-ards, was also not large, no doubt because the studios could not see putting major dollars into such an off-beat project.

Mimi Rogers, the remarkable star of *The Rapture*, plays a telephone operator whose job is repetitive and mind-numbing as she sits in a cubicle next to dozens of other operators and spends only seconds on each call. But by night she and her male friend Vic (Patrick Bauchau) pick up couples in bars and then engage in group sex. One night they pick up a couple in a bar, the man played by Duchovny with long hair. They go to Vic's furniture store where Mimi Rogers says "Vic likes to watch." "Watch this," says Randy (Duchovny) and then proceeds to have sex with both women. There is a taut, laconic quality to his acting and an intense, philosophical and yet almost dangerous qual-ity to his character that gives his performance real power. During the sex scenes his young, well-built body has a rare elegance to it.

Despite those sex scenes *The Rapture* is not a por-nographic film in any sense and the ominous tone prevents it from being really erotic. The viewer senses that Mimi Rogers' character is emotionally bankrupt and on the desperate edge of some imminent break-down. After failing to commit suicide, she finds herself attracted to a Christian fundamentalist cult and one day she tosses Randy out of bed and strips off the "unclean" sheets. Randy tries to convince her that she is being fooled by faith and that there is no God, only chaos. Duchovny conveys these difficult lines (difficult because of their intellectual seriousness) with subtle conviction.

The film jumps six years to show that Randy himself has been converted, that the two have married and now belong to the cult with their daughter. Randy's long hair has been cut conservatively and he wears a business suit. There is a solemn air to him now that is affecting. Not long after, a disgruntled employee at his business enters with a shot gun and kills several people, including Randy.

For the rest of the film the Mimi Rogers character becomes even more fanatical, kills her daughter as sacrifice, and ends up in prison. It is a shocking and disturbing film that attempts to grapple with troubling emotions and dangerous trends in American society, and even when it is not successful the attempt is admirable. The *New York Times* praised it warmly: "Mr. Tolkin has made a stark, daringly original film that viscerally demonstrates the courage of his convictions." While the critics understandably focused their attention on Mimi Rogers' performance, they also noted Duchovny with approval. It was also clear, however, that the subject matter would limit the film's potential success. As *Variety* put it, the "bizarre drama has little to offer mainstream audiences."

Duchovny found the shoot a difficult experience, no doubt because of the intensity of the script. It was also a role in which he appeared nude, as he did in *New Year's Day*, something that interviewers have repeatedly asked him about. His reply has been that if a part demands nudity then he will do it, even frontal nudity. "It's just a penis, you know," he has said, stating the obvious. In one of his more provocative moments he said, "While it's still young and relatively nice, I think I'll show [his behind] as much as I can."

On one of the many internet web sites devoted to
Duchovny and *The X-Files*, there is a page called "Sue's
Candid Movie Reviews." Sue is one of Duchovny's
many female fans and her critique of *The Rapture* is
both amusing and annoying: "Do you want to see
[Duchovny] doing two women at once? Do you want
to watch him give a hand job to Mimi Rogers (under
the covers)? . . . Do you want to see [Duchovny] get
shot in the chest? Then this movie is for you." It is
annoying because Duchovny's fans, preferring to fawn
over his good looks, have not always taken his acting
seriously. They tend to concentrate on silly details
(such as noting all his nude scenes) without noticing
that both he and the film are trying to do something
meaningful and serious. Duchovny himself seems to
be aggravated by this small-mindedness.

THE WORKING LIFE

How many films can one actor be in during a single year? The year 1992 saw Duchovny in no less than six films for theatrical release and television, although only one was a leading role. If he wasn't yet a star, or even playing the parts he wanted, he certainly didn't have to rely on his friends to pay the rent any more.

In *Chaplin*, Richard Attenborough's bio-pic, Duchovny played a close friend of the silent film star. Unfortunately, the movie was a box-office failure and the critics complained of its hurried and superficial treatment of the subject. (Only Robert Downey Jr. was praised for his convincing portrait of Chaplin.) A much less ambitious but much more successful film was *Beethoven*, a children's picture about a big and

sloppy Saint Bernard. This time Duchovny got to play
an evil yuppie, one of his rare bad-guy roles, and the
director, Brian Levant, encouraged his actors to play
their parts in a broad, cartoonish manner. Duchovny
did not seem to be particularly fond of the real pooch.
"He had a lot of saliva," Duchovny said. "Saint Bernard saliva is sticky and nasty. If you can imagine
bad-smelling maple sap, that's what it's like to work
with that dog."

One of the actresses on the shoot who became a
friend of Duchovny's, Bonnie Hunt, felt much more
positively about working with *him*. "The sexy thing
about David is his mind," she said afterwards.

Duchovny also appeared as part of the ensemble
cast in another Henry Jaglom film, this one called
Venice / Venice. Once again Jaglom played a role, as a
film-maker at the Venice Film Festival. But the critics
found it too self-absorbed and irritating and it received
less attention than other recent Jaglom films.

Duchovny played his second police officer in *Ruby*,
a not-much-seen movie about Jack Ruby, the killer of
Lee Harvey Oswald that starred Danny Aiello. Duchovny
must have been remembering his father's play about
Oswald when he made it. But the true embarrassment
of 1992 was a television movie with the unappealing
crisis-of-the-week title of *Baby Snatcher*. After becoming a star on *The X-Files* Duchovny preferred to forget
that he had ever done this one.

LOVE, SEX, AND
REALLY NICE CLOTHES

Zalman King is the crown prince of respectable soft-porn movies. He began as an actor, studying with Stella Adler in New York and then finding guest roles on such shows as *Bonanza* and *Gunsmoke*. In 1970 he starred in a television series called *The Young Lawyers*. Later he became a director, and in 1986 he and his wife Louisiana Knop co-wrote and produced *9½ Weeks*, the soft-porn sadomasochistic film starring Mickey Rourke that has made over $100 million worldwide. The couple followed up with *Wild Orchard*.

The critics have hated King's films, calling them dull, silly, and not even very erotic, but King and Knop have defended them as sincere explorations of the complexities of love and desire. At the age of fifty, King sold a film idea to the pay TV channel Showtime. It would be called *The Red Shoe Diaries*.

No doubt it was Duchovny's good looks more than his acting ability that got him the role of a successful architect in love with a young pixie of a woman, played by Brigitte Bako. As the film opens, Duchovny, beautifully dressed and sorrowful looking, attends the funeral for his girlfriend who has just committed suicide. Returning to their apartment (an enormous fantasy loft lit by shadows) he finds a pair of red shoes and a journal. In the journal the dead woman wrote about an affair she had, which is shown in a series of flashbacks. Apparently the Duchovny character was just too perfect and she couldn't bear it. The man with whom she has an affair is a construction worker and in a less than subtle symbolic moment she first sees him using a powerful jackhammer, breaking a pipe so that a burst of water shoots up into the air. (The man is also a part-time shoe salesman — thus the red shoes.)

The film shows Duchovny looking forlorn or, in flashbacks, meeting the woman's tough-as-nails mother, running with his love through the tall grass, standing by enormous models of his buildings, or having sex. Most of the time he seems to be posing in his handsome wardrobe. It is hard to imagine any viewer not finding it trite, pretentious, mannered, and excruciatingly dull. Those waiting for the explicit scenes have to wait a long time, only to be disappointed. Nevertheless, the film was successful enough to be turned into an ongoing series.

The real star of the film was Brigitte Bako, who had to run a gamut of incredible emotions, dance about wildly, and allow the camera to caress her nymph-like body. She reported afterwards that Zalman King was a tyrant on the set, intense and "absolutely brutal." Several times she broke down and cried between takes. Duchovny, on the other hand, considered the shoot one of the most important for his early development as an actor. He felt that for the first time he was getting a firm sense of his traits and abilities. It is hard to understand why, considering the poor quality of the film. Perhaps it was because King allowed him to play the role without large emotions or histrionics (they were left for Bako), but with more subtle expressions of feeling. Perhaps it was King's background as a student of Stella Adler, the same famous method-acting coach who had been Henry Jaglom's teacher;

King's style might have reminded Duchovny of his old teacher, Martha Haufrecht. Nor was he at all embarrassed by the explicit scenes. "I have never found sex scenes embarrassing," he said, "and I don't think they're hard to do either."

Trashy or not, *Red Shoe Diaries* helped to raise Duchovny's public profile. And when it became a Saturday-night series on Showtime, with Duchovny acting as host and occasional player, it also provided him with an easy and sizeable paycheck. He would shoot six episodes in a single day, his "Jack Nicholson" day he would call it because of the money he was being paid for so little work. Not being one to mince words, he did not call the show a "romance" as some did euphemistically, but the more accurate "soft-core pornography."

A STARRING ROLE

One day, when Duchovny is an old man, he will hardly be able to reminisce about all those years in B-movies and bit parts before finally getting his big break. These smaller roles and small-budget films quickly led to a starring role in what the industry likes to call "a major motion picture." Polygram Film and Viacom were the producing studios for *Kalifornia*, and Dominic Sena was the director. Once more Duchovny would find himself in an unusual film; the screenplay by Tim Metcalfe was a dark, violent road picture through the underbelly of America.

The film would be almost completely dominated by its four principal actors and the casting director, Carol

Lewis, knew the importance of choosing the right players. Duchovny and the actress Michelle Forbes would play the "normal" couple and Juliette Lewis and Brad Pitt their twisted companions. Pitt was the biggest name among the four, a young heart-throb actor who was quickly gaining fans. Juliette Lewis had also had some major roles, including one in Woody Allen's *Husbands and Wives*.

In the film, which was released in 1993, Duchovny plays Brian, a liberal-minded magazine writer who believes that murderers are mentally ill and shouldn't be executed. His girlfriend Carrie is a stylish photographer who takes Mapplethorpe-like photographs of nude bodies engaged in sex. The couple live in a loft and wear chic black leather. Brian has an earring in his right ear and Carrie a cooly severe haircut and black underwear which she seems to walk around in a lot.

Brian decides to write about the sites of famous murders across America and Carrie agrees to take the photos as long as they end up in California. (The idea that a publisher might produce a coffee-table book about murder seems rather farfetched, but no matter.) Because they don't have much money Brian advertises for someone to share the driving expenses. What they get is Juliette Lewis and Brad Pitt.

Lewis and Pitt play a backwoods, uneducated "Okie" couple named Adele and Early who seemed to have walked out of a depression dustbowl. "White trash" is how Carrie describes them. She is suspicious of Early from the beginning, but Brian never seems to catch on and instead claims she's prejudiced. Indeed, the mild intellectual Brian is drawn to the down-home anarchic energy and dangerous masculinity of the scruffy, ill-mannered Early. The audience, how-ever, has already seen that Early is a killer and on the back roads of America things begin to go wrong. Early murders along the way and when his crimes are discovered he takes Brian and Carrie hostage. After killing his girlfriend Adele, he leaves Brian in hand-cuffs and escapes with Carrie as his prisoner, who he rapes. But Brian gets loose and after finding them the audience is subjected to the inevitable bloody and horrifying showdown in which Brian finds out what it feels like to kill someone instead of just write about it.

In the film Duchovny draws on the repressed acting style to good effect. In his voiceovers can be heard a hint of the Fox Mulder character: intelligent, thought-ful, pained. If there is a fault in his character it is mostly in the writing, which does not examine his attraction to violence very far. Certainly the most extraordinary performance comes from Juliette Lewis and it is hard to believe that the same young actress who played a brainy and upper-class private-school girl in *Husbands and Wives* could transform herself into the ignorant, needy, and awkward Adele. Duchovny is well aware that as an actor he has never made this kind of leap, transforming himself into a totally different being. Compared to Pitt and Lewis, he was (and is) still in an early stage of his acting development.

But what is most interesting about *Kalifornia* is the way that the casting director sensed something in Duchovny that made him right for the part of Brian. In a eerie way the role he plays metaphorically paral-lels his own life and career. Like the character of Brian who is drawn to Early, Duchovny is an analytical and intellectual person who has found himself drawn to that other, more visceral and seductive side of the personality that is represented by acting. Rather than being about a murderer, *Kalifornia* is really about a repressed individual who faces his wilder and more dangerous self. There is a memorable scene in the film where Early coaxes the uptight Brian to try shooting his gun at an abandoned house. At first Brian refuses — liberals don't approve of guns — but finally he gives in and when his shot shatters a window he shouts as gleefully as a young boy. But as the film's climax crudely shows, loosening the reigns of repression sometimes unleashes uncontrollable forces.

The film's shoot was a tough one, with a lot of physical work to do, and the cast and crew had to travel to the various sites. Duchovny had that experience of feeling like he was working with a new family. Brad Pitt turned out to be a very reserved person and Duchovny speculated that all of the press attention, especially in the tabloid papers, must have been emotionally difficult for him. It was a premonition of what Duchovny himself would receive in the form of public attention.

Unfortunately, *Kalifornia* did not do much business at the box office. Most likely its less than likeable characters and realistic violence turned the audience away. A year after the film's release Duchovny would attend the Golden Globe Awards where, to everyone's surprise, *The X-Files* would beat out *ER* and *NYPD Blue* for best dramatic series. Duchovny was glad the show was being considered a drama rather than just a science-fiction show; to him that gave it more class. Not surprisingly, he was feeling pretty cocky that night as he took his turn fielding reporters' questions. A reporter asked not about his own career but what it had been like to work with Brad Pitt, who had been named by *People* magazine as the "sexiest man alive." His ego deflated, Duchovny replied that he had tried to learn how to be sexy by watching Pitt.

SIX

BECOMING MULDER

Until now Duchovny had almost always been cast in roles with a strong sexual component. For instance, in *Kalifornia* he had to simulate having sex with Michelle Forbes against a motel wall while Brad Pitt listened on the other side. Perhaps directors simply felt there was a strong sensual quality to his good looks. But the role that would make him famous would give Duchovny no sex scenes at all, and at least for a while it would be a refreshing change.

Duchovny and his agent agreed that he had a chance for stardom and should pursue a career in movies rather than television. But one day the agent sent

Duchovny a script for a television pilot, the only television project that he would send him that season. It was the quality of the writing for a show with the odd name *The X-Files* that appealed to him.

The author of the script, who was also the show's executive producer, was a not-very-well-known quantity named Chris Carter. Raised in Bellflower, California, he had begun his career after graduating from California State University by editing *Surfing* magazine for several years. It was his wife, Dori Pierson, a screenwriter herself, who convinced him to try writing scripts. He was soon hired by Disney's Jeffrey Katzenberg and turned out such fare as *B.R.A.T. Patrol* and *Meet the Munceys*. After that he went to NBC, where he wrote several pilots and tried to develop such shows as *Rags to Riches*, a musical comedy, and *Copter Cop*, a science fiction show, without much success. Then in 1992 Peter Roth, who had recently become president of TV production at Twentieth Century–Fox, hired Carter as a producer on the strength of his writing ability. Until that point Carter had succeeded most by writing comedy, but his real love was for dark fright dramas on the order of *Kolchak: The Night Stalker* and *The Twilight Zone* which he had watched as a kid.

As the relatively new fourth network, Fox had done well with such sitcoms as *Married . . . With Children*, but had never managed a hit one-hour drama series. Carter was in his mid-thirties, a handsome man with an open and pleasant face, silvery hair flowing to his shoulders, and perfect white teeth — an ex-surfer radiating good health. He had come up with a show about an FBI agent assigned to x-file cases, unexplained phenomena such as UFOs, alien sightings, strange creatures, and even ghosts. The agent had a special interest in such cases as he believed that his own sister had been abducted by aliens when they were children. But certain powerful figures in the government and the agency did not want this information released. And so the agent would have to do battle not only with these strange forces but also with a conspiracy within his own organization.

Duchovny agreed with his agent that the pilot script for *The X-Files* was of superior quality and even though he wasn't interested in doing a series he thought that it might be good work and another step for his career. In all likelihood, Duchovny reasoned, the pilot wouldn't get picked up (most pilots don't) and even if it did it would probably only run for six shows before cancellation. A show about UFOS — "alien-of-the-week" he called it — seemed rather limited to him and the show appeared more of an anthology (each show barely related to the others) than a true continuing series. He did not predict either the variety of subjects the show would tackle or that the developing history of the characters of Mulder and Scully would hold an audience's attention.

The audition went well; Chris Carter immediately knew that he had found Fox Mulder. "David Duchovny was an early favourite and he was an easy person to cast," Carter said afterwards. "He fit the character I had written very well and he played it with a — he underplayed it is what he did and I think it won him the part. Also he has a tremendous amount of personal magnetism and sex appeal." Casting the role of Agent Scully, the female doctor who would be assigned to Mulder to act as the voice of reason and disbelief, proved to be more difficult and callbacks were necessary. He soon settled on a young actress named Gillian Anderson with virtually no experience in front of a camera; she had only had one guest role in a single television show.

Now in her early twenties, Anderson was a former punk-rock groupie who had acted in New York theater before moving to L.A. in the hope of breaking into film and television. At the callback Duchovny approached her and asked if he could read with her in front of Carter and the network brass. The reading went extremely well; Duchovny took on a sarcastic edge that Anderson reacted to with natural defensiveness, giving her reading just the right tone. Carter was convinced but the network didn't want her. They wanted a star, someone who would draw curious viewers from the start. Also, they wanted a more obvious knock-out beauty, someone "leggier" and "with more breasts" as Anderson later put it. But Carter held his ground and they gave in.

Later Anderson would praise the "warmth and intelligence" that Duchovny brought to the role of Mulder. "I don't think anybody in their right mind could not find him attractive." She would also express her appreciation for how the more experienced actor took her "under his wing," reassuring her and helping her through the frightening experience of filming the first episodes.

After winning the Mulder role, Duchovny had to sign the standard agreement before filming of the pilot began. The contract obliged him to a set number of years playing the character should the show be a success. Did Duchovny realize what he was getting himself into? asked his agent. After all, Duchovny had wanted to become a movie star, moving from part to part. Duchovny said he did understand, but in retrospect he would realize how naïve he had been. He did not appreciate either the work load on a television series or the frustration and monotony of playing the same character for years. He just thought it was another job.

THE PILOT

In the pilot episode, Duchovny's character does not make his introduction for several minutes. Instead the audience meets Scully and finds out about her assignment to work with — or rather try to neutralize — Agent Mulder. Thus in a manner perhaps not absolutely clear, the viewer is invited to share Scully's point of view. The first time Mulder is seen is from the back, examining a slide in his basement office. Without turning around he speaks his first line: "Sorry, nobody down here but the FBI's most unwanted."

The murder of several high-school classmates in Oregon has got Mulder hot under the collar. From the start, Duchovny as Mulder charms even as he persuades Scully (and the audience) of his convictions. He banters intellectually, hair falling over his eye. That his voice is not strong and even sounds occasionally garbled contributes to his moody, loner quality. Duchovny must deliver a lot of information in his speeches, from scientifically-grounded information to far-fetched speculation, and he does so convincingly.

Perhaps his time as a university instructor helped in his delivery of these souped-up lectures on the paranormal. But he also shows his touch for humor, such as the moment when he knocks on Scully's motel door and, when she asks who it is, replies, "Steven Spielberg."

While the pilot's story-line was not without holes, it nevertheless provided for a compelling hour of drama and the establishing of the relationship of Scully and Mulder as well as the ominous role of their FBI superiors. There was a rich feature-film look to it, partly as a result of shooting outdoors in the Vancouver area. Viewers who tuned in would no doubt be intrigued enough to watch again.

As the series went on Duchovny would often be asked whether he himself believed in UFOs and alien life. No reporter seemed to consider this an odd question, even though actors who play, say, murderers or inventors are never asked if they would like to murder someone or have actually invented anything. In early interviews he simply said no but after a while, perhaps out of boredom, he began to soften this opinion, saying that there was no reason that earth should be the only planet with life. Once he even mentioned seeing a UFO in 1982 in Ocean City, New Jersey. Occasionally his impatience with the question showed. When asked why aliens have never landed in Times Square, he replied, "I hate to do the thinking for the aliens."

Clearly though, Duchovny did not need to believe in order to get inside the role of Fox Mulder. Sometimes he did not really understand the speeches he was required to give with such intense conviction.

A WARY ROMANCE

After making *Kalifornia* and the pilot episode of *The X-Files*, Duchovny felt at least a bit more economically secure. Friends convinced him to celebrate his growing success by buying a new suit (he hadn't had a new one for years) and so he went to Fred Segal's in Santa Monica. He was trying to choose between a blue and a grey suit when he noticed a beautiful woman shopping. She was slim, not tall, with long brown hair, and she was accompanied by an older woman who was likely her mother.

Wishing to speak to her, Duchovny asked for her opinion about the suits. She told him he ought to buy both. The woman was an actress named Perrey Reeves who was with her mother on a buying trip for lingerie (she refrained from asking Duchovny *his* opinion). Before long the two were a couple.

Duchovny found that Reeves was a private person and often quiet, in contrast to his tendency to want to tell everyone everything. She lived in Los Angeles and because he would have to spend most of the year in Vancouver, the two would see each other only on alternate weekends. During the second season he would get to act with her when she was cast as Kristen Kiler, a member of a vampire cult who he may or may not have had sex with (the possibility is left vague) before she dies in order to save him. Duchovny, who admitted that the episode (called "3") had too many lapses of logic, found it difficult to act opposite his girlfriend. Reeves, he said, was used to seeing him "defensive and uptight" the way he was in real life, and not honest and vulnerable as he became while acting.

The paparazzi would enjoy snapping photos of the couple for publication in the gossip magazines, and the two seemed a close and attractive couple. Vancouver and L.A. were two-and-a-half hours away by plane, however, and not living in the same city was a strain on the relationship. Perhaps not as great a strain, though, as Duchovny's own inability to make an emotional commitment. The wound of his parents' divorce had never really healed. "I guess I'll get married when I'm supposed to get married," he said unenthusiastically to one interviewer.

THE
FIRST
SEASON

Duchovny was wrong about *The X-Files*. The executives at Fox liked the pilot and gave Carter the green light for a first season. They began to film the first episodes — "Deep Throat," "Squeeze," "Conduit," and "The Jersey Devil."

At the beginning, the character of Mulder was somewhat vague. It was up to Duchovny to deepen and expand the role by understanding his own motivations and providing the character with more background. Like any actor, he had to imaginatively fill in the back story, bringing the character up to the point of time when the series took place. Sometimes a small detail can help focus an actor, such as Duchovny's decision that Mulder should wear funny ties. Otherwise Mulder was an intense and lonely figure, someone whose preoccupation had reduced the rest of his life to almost nothing. "The greatest thing about Mulder," Duchovny said, "is that he doesn't care what people think of him. But his big weakness is the same thing." He added, "The sad thing about Mulder is that he rarely gets to see what he wants to see. So he's one step behind. He only gets the smell of the alien or the slime of the alien or the hint of the alien."

But Duchovny also liked Mulder to have a sense of humor, often at Scully's expense. As the first season progressed he felt some dismay at the increase in the character's intensity and the decrease in wisecracks. But he was able to influence the scripts, such as the second-season episode with Perrey Reeves. When a vampire cult member asks him, "Don't you want to live forever?" Duchovny had Mulder reply, "Well, not if drawstring pants come back into style." At the same time, he hoped that the intensity would not merely be a matter of reacting to yet another bizarre phenomenon each week. He hoped that the writers would take Mulder on an "interior journey" of discovery and self-revelation.

The acting style that Duchovny brought to the part was more "instinctual" than analytical, he said. He felt that Mulder suffered from a kind of detachment from others while at the same time a deep attachment to his beliefs. Mulder reacted intellectually to events, with his head rather than his heart or sex drive, but underneath that rational surface was a person "constantly suppressing a great deal of sadness and pain."

This sounded a lot like the personality of Duchovny himself. Part of his job as an actor was to allow that pain a way to express itself in each show.

Duchovny believed that he brought a new, more subtle acting style to television, a medium not exactly known for subtlety. This acting style of repression has been occasionally criticized as an underplaying of the role, but Duchovny has insisted that most acting on television is simply unrealistic. Other critics have proved more perceptive. Jack Hitt, a television critic for *Playboy*, showed great insight when he wrote of Duchovny's minimalist acting style and compared him to an existential film-noir hero who believed that the best a person could do in this life "was conduct oneself with suspicious cool until the inexorable finale arrived from the muzzle of a gun or with a shove from a roof." In the same vein, one might use a literary equivalent and say that Duchovny acted the way Hemingway wrote, with direct, quiet, courageous grace. As an actor he might be compared to the stoicism of Clint Eastwood.

Another intelligent critic, writing in *Spectrum* magazine, described Duchovny's acting in the opening second-season episode this way: "In 'Little Green Men' [Duchovny] revealed — not as much through dialogue, but through subtle body language — his emotional and psychological suffering. . . ." The critic wrote of his "grim determination" in another episode and in yet another of the way he expressed not anger but "resignation, as if he would always be out-maneuvered by larger, more powerful forces."

On a practical level, acting in *The X-Files* brought its own challenges. How was Mulder supposed to respond to a six-foot-tall Cro-Magnon woman in "The Jersey Devil"? No matter how amazed he found himself in an episode, there was always a new level of astonishment that he was supposed to reach in the next. Because the special effects were usually not ready when the actors shot their scenes, they would have to react without knowing exactly what they were looking at. As a result Duchovny felt that he ended up overacting when seeing some UFOs in the sky that turned out to be a couple of small dots. At the other end of the scale, his reaction to the horrifying Fluke Man was almost flat. "There's no way that [the flat expression] was an appropriate reaction. In any universe," he said after seeing the finished episode. On another occasion he said, "It all boils down to projecting bigger or less emotions. I've basically to decide every week whether I'm up against the Holy Grail or the Shroud of Turin and then act accordingly."

GOOD IDEAS

Working on a television show is truly like adopting a new family; you sometimes love these people, you sometimes despise them, but either way you can't escape them. Duchovny was fortunate to find himself liking his fellow cast and crew members. He and Chris Carter hit it off and became close personal friends, playing squash together in their off hours. About his boss Duchovny said, "Chris Carter is great. He's the only person I know who works as hard as I do on the show. He just won't let it be any less than the best it can be and that's a spur for me to work hard." As long as Carter stayed involved in the show instead of moving on to other projects (as executive producers often do once a show is established), Duchovny was sure it would remain first-rate.

A plus in this friendship was that Carter turned out to be receptive to Duchovny's ideas about the show. Actors often contribute little bits of *shtick* or a line change here or there, but Duchovny would eventually help to develop some of the episodes' actual story lines. His experience as an English student and a would-be writer gave him a strong sense of language and the effects of narrative structure and he applied them to the show. In the first season his contribution was more modest but still significant. His purpose was almost always to make the character of Fox Mulder more interesting to play. Carter said simply, "He's got good ideas for the show. Why not use them?" At the beginning the two had what Duchovny called "a constant battle" about Mulder. Duchovny wanted to make him funnier and give a lighter tone to some of his lines, while Carter was obsessively concerned with not breaking the atmosphere of suspense. Duchovny also thought it was unrealistic for all of Mulder's motivations to be linked to the abduction of his sister; people just didn't guide their whole lives because of one moment. Sometimes Duchovny would get to influence the script and sometimes he wouldn't, but during the actual shooting there was little room to improvise because of the complicated plots that had to be worked through to their conclusions. "We're all slaves to the story," Duchovny said with obvious frustration.

Duchovny also managed to have some influence in the casting of guest actors. After reading the script for "The Jersey Devil," an episode that would air early in the first season, he immediately suggested that an actress named Claire Stansfield play the evolutionary throw-back. He and Stansfield had been friends since he had worked with her on *Twin Peaks* and her height (over six feet) as well as her attractive looks made her perfect for the role. Carter agreed. A lot of hair was needed from the make-up department to turn her into the "devil" (in part to cover her breasts) and the two friends had fun filming the episode. In one scene she had to straddle Duchovny wearing only a G-string and the two of them kept laughing.

Later in the first season an episode called "Darkness Falls" aired with Duchovny's oldest friend, Jason Beghe, playing the role of Forest Ranger Larry Moore. From the start Duchovny had kept an eye open for a part his friend could play, and once it was found Beghe did not even have to audition. The shoot proved unexpectedly difficult due to rain and snow and there were several delays. More delays resulted from the two friends cracking up on the set.

But the person who Duchovny most had to work with was Gillian Anderson. Relative to her, he was the veteran and continued to help and reassure her during the early episodes. "He was wonderful," was how she summarized her feelings. At the beginning Anderson had trouble memorizing and delivering some of Scully's lines, especially the ones loaded with medical and technical jargon. According to one crew member, Duchovny sometimes couldn't help becoming upset by her mistakes. He himself had no difficulty learning or performing his own long-winded speeches, some-times at break-neck speed. But fairly quickly they learned to trust each other, a necessity considering that each episode relied so heavily on them both and their working days were long and exhausting, often going into the early morning hours. And they became sensitive to how fatigue could make one or the other irritated or impatient. Although their friendship did not extend into the off-hours, it was genuine.

EIGHT

THE TRANSIENT

After *The X-Files* became a definite success in the second season, magazine writers would not be able to resist quoting the critic who predicted that the show would soon be pulled from the schedule. The reviewer at *People* would prove to have a more dependable crystal ball: "If the producers can keep the mood spooky, this show will have its devoted adherents." That turned out to be true enough, but even *People* didn't predict that the program would break the confines of cult status and reach a truly wide audience. Indeed, who could have predicted it, considering that the early ratings were middling at best?

Meanwhile, Duchovny quickly found the grind of putting out a weekly one-hour series that relied heavily on his screen presence to be exhausting. "I had never experienced that kind of load," he said later, comparing it to participating in a triathalon. "Year one was just about survival — am I *physically* going to survive?" During these long and often repetitive days it was the director's job to keep up the interest and intensity of the actors. But on the series, like most others, the director changed from episode to episode, adding to the strain. The first season employed over a dozen different directors and there was often no time to develop a relationship of trust so that Duchovny sometimes found himself feeling wary. One director he particularly liked was Rob Bowman, who was also a producer on the show and who praised the actor as "One-take Duchovny" for doing a scene right the first time the camera rolled. Another who Duchovny praised was David Nutter who directed several first-season episodes, including the notorious "Ice," Christ Carter's homage to the 1951 horror film *The Thing*.

Each episode usually had an eight-day shooting schedule, although near the end of the season some shows would get only six days. A lot of planning was done in order for the shoot to go smoothly, without time and cost over-runs. From pre-production to having the finished episode in the can would take from six to eight weeks and several episodes were always in the works at once, one being re-written, another prepped, a third shot, and a fourth in post-production. For Duchovny a day's shooting might last twelve hours and finish at 2 a.m., after which he would have the ninety-minute drive back to his house in Vancouver.

The show would have to shoot eight pages of script each work day, three or four times the amount a feature film would do. While a stunt man was used for the more dangerous work, he still had to do a lot of physical stuff. (For example, in the second season episode "Ascension" he would do his own stunts in the scenes on the aerial tram.) Because of the long hours he sometimes found it difficult to be "on" when called on to shoot a scene and there were some days when he just felt that he hadn't acted well. As well, his own preparation time was by necessity often minimal. He felt that this hurt his acting, even as he recognized that it forced him to use his instincts and not "agonize" over a scene.

At the same time, not all the work was as intense as it later appeared to viewers of the show. Sometimes the most dramatic moments were the ones where he and Anderson would break up with laughter, ruining the take. For example, in a second-season episode ("Dod Kalm") where they aged ninety years in two days they kept laughing at guest actor John Savage's delivery of a line in Norwegian. As well, some outtakes from the show have surfaced: a water fountain spritzing water into Duchovny's face (for "Die Hand Die Verletzt"); Duchovny wading through a flooded hallway and ad-libbing, "This is my hot tub in my trailer. I have a big star contract" (for "Excelsis Dei").

When not being called on for a shot, Duchovny spent most of his time in his trailer listening to *The Rolling Stones* or *The Beatles* or reading the latest Martin Amis novel. It wasn't long before he had a companion for company, a part border collie mutt who was the offspring of a dog used in one of the episodes. Duchovny named her Blue after the Bob Dylan song, "Tangled Up in Blue," because he thought she would help take away some of his own sadness. He would bring Blue to the set every day and while she watched her owner act the crew members would stop to give her a pat. Later it would become a favorite plaything of Piper, Gillian Anderson's baby. As Duchovny's fame increased so did Blue's and a description of her would appear in national and international magazines, as well as some silly misinformation, such as the report that Blue had a special liking for licking feet. (In fact, Blue did lick Duchovny's feet during a phone interview, from which the story originated, but she never did it again. On *The Tonight Show* Duchovny would say to Jay Leno with a serious expression, "This caused a lot of pain in my family.")

In an odd way Duchovny's devotion to the dog was another sign of his difficulty in making emotional commitments. "Love is much easier to give to a dog than to a person," he admitted. And as *Seventeen* magazine reported, he spent his free time with girlfriend Perrey Reeves and with Blue, "not necessarily in that order."

LONELY IN LOTUSLAND

The province of British Columbia, and its principal city of Vancouver, are home to many television shows and film shoots. Not only is it relatively less expensive to make a show in Canada than in the U.S., but B.C. has a tremendous variety of settings within a reasonable distance — water, bridges, forests, and urban streets. It can double for many places, a great advantage for a show like *The X-Files* which sends Mulder and Scully all over the United States.

British Columbia is often called Lotusland, but this apparent paradise seemed something less than ideal to Duchovny. He had to spend ten months out of the year in Vancouver filming *The X-Files* and while he found the city beautiful, the cold and rainy weather did not appeal to him after California. He rented a small, simple house over eighty years old on the ocean because of the beautiful view. The windows looked out on the bay and the mountains beyond. Wooden stairs took him down to the beach which was not sandy as in California, but rocky and with seaweed drifting in the shallows. In the morning he would take Blue for a walk, work out, go over the latest script. On his off hours he would nip into a Starbucks for hot cider, go to a health food place near the pool where he went swimming called the Yam Café. Almost a vegetarian, he was careful about eating and exercising in order to stay healthy. If he should get too sick to work, production of the show would have to shut down, costing tens of thousands of dollars.

Worst of all about living in Vancouver was simple loneliness. He had no real connections there, no family or old friends. It was like living in the place you work and never going home. When the show went into hiatus between seasons he would rent a place back in California, such as a beach house in Malibu. But these short stays didn't feel like home either. "I'm a transient," he would sigh. "Most of my life takes place on the inside. Nothing much sticks to me."

One day during the winter of the first season Gillian Anderson came into Duchovny's trailer and closed the door. "David," she said, "I'm pregnant."

"Oh my God," he responded. He asked her if she was glad about the pregnancy and she said yes. That, at least, was a relief. But what about the show? She asked Duchovny to keep her secret for a while and he agreed, a mark of trust between them.

When Chris Carter fought to cast Anderson in the rule of Dana Scully he was not worrying about the possibility of his star becoming pregnant. In fact, Anderson wasn't even married. But after the show began she quickly became involved with a Canadian named Clyde Klotz who was working as the production designer. They decided to marry suddenly — the wedding vows took place on a golf course in Hawaii — and the child was conceived at about the same time.

Duchovny kept the secret for several weeks but finally Anderson had to tell Carter. Some inside sources have reported that Carter went "ballistic"; here he finally had the show he wanted on the air and one of his stars decided this was the time to become a mother! In his anger he considered replacing her with another actress. Carter himself claims that this response never happened and that he has always supported Anderson.

In the end, the decision was made to keep Anderson on the show, but it would mean a radical rethinking of plot lines for the second season, when the baby was due. How could they keep the pregnancy hidden and what would they do for the shows which Anderson would have to miss? Rumors circulated among *X-Files* fans that a plot line was being developed in which Anderson was impregnated by an alien life form. New viewers would tune in just to see what happens.

INVASION OF THE CYBER-GROUPIES

While the first-year ratings of *The X-Files* were not brilliant — something over six million households tuned in for most of the season — they were respectable. By the season's end they would begin to rise; the last episode, "The Erlenmeyer Flask," would draw almost eight million households. Almost from the beginning, though, the show attracted hardcore fans who, being computer literate, began to talk to one another via the internet. They set up web sites and compiled information about the show and its stars, as well as giving themselves a forum for discussion. It wouldn't be long before there were dozens of internet sites and newsgroups devoted to *The X-Files*, many in such countries as Norway, France, and even in Malaysia where the show would also be aired.

Among these fans were several groups of women crazy about David Duchovny. Two of them, the "David Duchovny Estrogen Brigade," and the "Duchovnicks," would close off membership in their groups because there were too many messages about their idol for anyone to respond to. They described his looks as "pure poetry," used short-forms such as WPDF

("Wounded Puppy Dog Face") and c & v ("Cute and Vulnerable"), gathered information about his career, sent each other excited messages whenever Duchovny took of his shirt or appeared in a Speedo bathing suit in an episode. The fans themselves became an item for the press, with the *New York Times* calling Duchovny "the first internet sex symbol with hair." This was a reference to Patrick Stewart of *Star Trek* who had similar sites devoted to him.

Chris Carter was highly aware of these fans and even used the name of three members of the Brigade on an airline passenger flight manifest in the second season's opener, "Little Green Men." In another episode, "One Breath," one of the Lone Gunmen tells Mulder that he should join them on the internet on Friday night "to nitpick the scientific inaccuracies on *Earth 2*." Mulder replies: "I'm doing my laundry." In part this was the show's response to those people who used the internet to act as back-seat directors and find little flaws in the plots or criticize such trivial details as Scully not adjusting her car seat when taking over the driving from Mulder. But Mulder's reply might also have been Duchovny's. He was rather wary of this attention, just as he had mixed feelings about fame in general. He didn't check the internet himself to see what they were up to, figuring it would just make him feel lousy rather than good about himself. He drew on a German philosopher for his explanation: "Nietzsche says we remember what gives us pain." When asked about it he would say that he was merely an excuse for people to talk to each other about their lives, which was partly true. The fans, though, kept wanting him to "appear" on an internet talk show, in which people can send questions to a guest through their own computers. While he kept putting off such an appearance, saying he didn't like to be pressured or coerced, he did finally make one in January 1995. He had time only to say hello to all the "callers."

That's not to say that Duchovny tried to avoid being a sex symbol. He knew that his good looks had helped him succeed as an actor and no matter what misgivings he had about that fact he sometimes liked to milk it for all it was worth. During one appearance on *The Tonight Show* he suddenly pulled his shirt open, causing the women in the audience to go berserk. (When Jay Leno pointed out that this "alien gig" was a good way to meet women, Duchovny replied that whenever he flashed his FBI badge women have to obey: "They are legally bound by the U.S. Government to do what I want.") At other appearances he would talk about all the erotic mail he received.

During the first year of the show, Duchovny and some of the other members of the *X-Files* production team made a visit to the real FBI headquarters in New York. (The one in the show is actually the Vancouver office of the Canadian Broadcasting Corporation.) Duchovny toured the building and saw their technically advanced methods for solving crimes. Instead of being larger than life, he found the agents just "cops in civilian clothing," very professional, normal people. He did discover that, like Mulder, real agents like to wear funny ties. To his surprise the agents told him that they considered Mulder a good role model since he was polite and respectful to the people he spoke with.

The show's ratings placed it an unimpressive 102 out of 118 network shows. But because of the good word of mouth that was spreading about the show as well as praise from television critics as the season went on, Fox decided to renew the series. (Besides, their other drama, a western called *The Adventures of Briscoe County Jr*, had done much worse.) By the end of the season Duchovny was only being recognized on the street occasionally — his life had not yet been transformed. His opinion of the show's cult status was rather sceptical. He called it "fanaticism" resulting from viewers' fears the show would be cancelled and their desire to be able to say that they had discovered it first. Duchovny himself was already beginning to grow restless in the role of Fox Mulder. He hoped to shoot a movie during the off-season, comparing his desire to play another role to a married man wanting to have an affair. (Duchovny often likes to use sexual metaphors, which only adds to his aura of sexuality that some fans feel.) Unfortunately, the scheduling couldn't be worked out, so for now he was only Mulder.

NINE

LIFE
IS NOT
TELEVISION

What David Duchovny's female fans have called his wounded puppy dog look was a reduction of his real and brooding character. Like Samuel Beckett, the author he chose to write about as an undergraduate, Duchovny had a dark existential sense of life's absurdity. He spoke about how life was not like television, in which he got to shoot a scene over several times until it was right. Life was passing by without him really able to understand what it meant.

And life had brought him to this moment, when he was on the very cusp of major fame and life would seem even more absurdist and beyond his control.

Perhaps everyone has a hard time knowing who he or she is; our identities are surprisingly slippery and elusive and many people spend their lives in a fruitless quest to "know" themselves. It wasn't very long ago that Duchovny had reinvented himself, changing from intellectual academic to highly paid actor, a metamorphosis that would put anyone's sense identity into a serious spin.

His personality, at least that part of it that could be pinned down, was by turns introspective and extroverted. At parties and gatherings he was not a leader of talk or the centre of attention. He preferred to linger on the edge, listening and observing and only occasionally dropping in his own shrewd or witty comments. He was too self-deprecating to fully enjoy the limelight. His problem, or so he thought, was that he cared too much about what the world thought of him. This concern made him overly self-conscious and made him feel alienated from his true self. Because of this he was attracted to Zen, but he called what he believed a "fake Zen approach to life." The Zen approach was to be passionately detached, a contradiction hard to achieve, and one that Duchovny worked at desultorily without success. In a Zen-like manner he wanted to be rid of caring what anybody else thought of him. "The ultimate freedom is in not giving a shit," he said in his characteristic mix of high-flown and low-brow language.

Possibly it was this unsatisfied sense of himself that made him so suspicious of his own considerable intellect. While he would quote Dante or some difficult philosopher when speaking to newspaper reporters who aren't generally up on German thinkers or modern literature, he would also dismiss this knowledge and what it had given him. One could never learn important things about life from books, he insisted, but only from living and making mistakes.

The result of this confused desire not to care, his need to make people like him, his intelligence and his dismissal of it, is someone who often sent out very mixed messages to the outside world. In interviews he could be unguarded in his comments, often racy, but he could also pull back into sudden privacy. Unlike most people in the industry he was not afraid to speak his mind. For example, when one interviewer suggested that some people considered *The X-Files* to be more documentary than fiction, Duchovny replied, "There are people who think *Melrose Place* is true. That's a much scarier prospect." In the same fashion he was never afraid to name the episodes of his own show that he thought were inferior ("Ghost in the Machine" and "Lazarus" in the first year) or to joke that he thought the third season would be of high quality "before we slide back into mediocrity."

At other times he would simply become a big ham, hungry to please, and to do so he made use of his considerable sense of humor. He appeared on *The Late Show with David Letterman* after being bumped the night before and told the audience that Letterman had put him up for the night in his home, cooking him dinner, reading him a bedtime story, and tucking him into bed. On a later appearance he told Letterman that he had hoped to make his entrance riding on Ed Asner's back. On *The Tonight Show* he described how the French are dissatisfied with the lack of sex on *The X-Files* and so

whenever a woman walks by Mulder they have the
actor dubbing him go "Mmmmm."

As for ordinary daily life, Duchovny liked playing
squash and basketball when he could and followed his
favourite team, the Knicks. Although he had little time
to watch television, he preferred highly realistic
shows like *ER* or *Homicide* and seemed to envy the wide
range of scenes the actors got to play, from high drama
to comedy to small domestic moments. He practised
yoga, no doubt to further his desire for Zen-like
detachment, ran or swam for exercise, visited an acu-
puncturist on occasion, and loved taking baths. He was
crazy about contemporary music as he had been as a
kid and bought so many CDs he wondered if it was an
addiction. Among the groups he liked was Simply Red;
his favourite song of all time was "Thank You" by Sly
and the Family Stone. He had a historical sense of
popular music and criticized people these days for not
caring about originality and authenticity in music. Too
many people, he said, listened to the Red Hot Chili
Peppers "because they never heard of Jimi Hendrix."
Unlike Mulder who always wore suits, he preferred
jeans, black shirts, wrinkled clothes.

Not surprisingly, interviewers were highly aware of
his growing sex-symbol status and liked to ask him
questions about his own sexual preferences and ideas
about relationships. While still seeing Perrey Reeves
he said, "I do believe in monogamy. Some people have
it in their bones — it's their calling. But for others,
including me, staying monogamous requires constant
vigilance." He sounded an awful lot like a reformed
version of the character he played in *New Year's Day*.
On a lighter note, when asked by *Playgirl* what was

his favourite part of a woman he gave a sensual and unusual response: "The part right where the back of the upper thigh turns into the rear end. It's soft. It's fragrant. It's got everything you need. You could just build a house there and be happy."

That was the sort of answer that did little to dampen the spirits of those who saw Duchovny as a kind of intellectually superior sexual animal. And it was just one of the ways that he was learning to present himself to a world which seemed to want to know more and more about him.

TEN

THE SECOND SEASON SURGE

At the start of the second season *The X-Files* was largely considered by the industry to be a cult show. Fans were in the minority but their loyalty to the program was strong and they would even stay in on Fridays, normally a night with a smaller viewing audience, in order to watch it.

But during the second year the ratings began climbing right from the season opener, "Little Green Men," which had over nine million television sets tuned to it. Word had spread and people had caught enough reruns during the summer to want to tune in. During the season's most-watched episode, "Fresh Bones," the number would pass ten million — a particularly high number given that the show was on Fox, the network with the fewest affiliate stations. The show's share of the viewing audience increased by 44 percent, more than any other network series on the air.

For the most part Duchovny found the work easier. He was used to it for one thing, and now that the routine was set, the production was more organized and he even got the occasional day off. At the same time, it still consumed most of his life, leaving time for very little else. But he was pleased with the maturation of the stories. "We really became the best show on television," he boasted.

Duchovny himself was growing more famous — and more recognizable — literally week by week. Articles about him and the show began appearing in hundreds of newspapers and magazines. One day a production assistant came up to Duchovny on the set and said, "Robin Williams would like to meet you." "Oh no he wouldn't," Duchovny replied, thinking that someone was playing a joke. Then he heard Williams' voice say, "Oh yes he would."

During the off season the show's writers, headed by Chris Carter, had been planning for Gillian Anderson's temporary disappearance from the show as the date of expectancy grew closer. For the shoots early in the season a bed was kept on the set so that Anderson could rest between takes. Making an opportunity of necessity, they came up with a story line that produced some of the most acclaimed episodes of the series and that advanced the "mythology" of the show, as Carter called its continuing story arc. On October 14, 1994, the episode "Duane Barry" aired, a two-parter in which Scully is kidnapped by a former FBI agent who claims to have been repeatedly abducted by aliens. In the second part, "Ascension," the former agent Barry claims to have given Scully to the aliens in place of him; whatever did happen, Scully has disappeared. Then came the only episode that Anderson missed being in, the vampire story called "3." No doubt it was Scully's absence that prompted the writers to allow Mulder to have this one sexual encounter. Carter was adamant about Mulder and Scully continuing to have a strictly working relationship, and Duchovny whole-heartedly agreed, even if it was only natural for the two to look longingly at one another on occasion.

The story of Scully's apparent abduction was picked up in the following episode, "One Breath," in which she turned up in a hospital in a coma. (The coma allowed Anderson to lie down and even doze during the shoot. She returned to the set just days after giving birth to a girl by Cesarean section and was still taking fluids intravenously to regain her strength.) This series of episodes furthered the conspiracy theme of the show (the evil Krycek and the Cigarette-Smoking Man even discussed the possibility of killing Mulder) and helped to further the emotional bond of Mulder with Scully, whose abduction could not but remind him of the pain of losing his sister to aliens all those years ago.

"STORY BY DAVID DUCHOVNY"

Duchovny thought that the abduction-of-Scully episodes were among the best so far. He had strong tastes about the writing on the show; among his favourite writers was the team of Glen Morgan and James Wong. But Wong and Morgan would leave *The X-Files* to create a new show for Fox now that the network was heady with the success of *The X-Files* and hungry for more. (Alas, the show, called *Space*, would be short-lived.)

From the beginning of the series, Duchovny took an active interest in the stories that were told in each episode. His co-star Anderson was amazed at his ability to analyze a narrative and see its strengths and weaknesses. While Duchovny's own ambitions to write were frustrated by his heavy work load, his imagination did not become dormant. One day he went up to Carter and told him that he had an idea for an episode. After hearing it, Carter said that an idea of his own might fit nicely with Duchovny's, and together the two began to develop the story. One episode turned out to be too short to contain their ideas as they expanded; it would have to be a two-parter. They turned the story-line over to one of the show's writers, Frank Spotnitz, who turned it into scripts for the episodes "Colony" and "End Game." ("End Game" also happens to be the title of a play by Beckett.) In them an alien bounty hunter came to earth to kill off some fellow aliens trying to establish a colony and who have the ability to clone human forms. One form they clone is that of Mulder's sister, who he takes to be the real person. (Later when they tell him that his sister is still alive Mulder says, "I want to believe," a line that is often cited wrongly to mean he wants to believe in alien forms generally. What Mulder wants to believe is that his sister is alive.)

While Duchovny received a story credit along with Carter, he played down his involvement, noting that he didn't actually write the script. In fact, he admitted that the idea of writing the script was frightening to him; what if he had tried and failed, proving that he wasn't a writer after all? His acting schedule gave him no time to find out whether he could do it or not and later he mused that his life was already so tied up with the show it would probably be better to write something else when he had the time.

By the end of the season Fox had a bonafide dramatic hit. It had broken out from its cult status and David Duchovny's visibility as a star had soared. Both Duchovny's and Gillian Anderson's management asked to renegotiate their stars' contracts and the two received impressive salary increases. This is normal Hollywood business — when a show is successful the agents start picking up their phones. As Chris Carter said, Duchovny and Anderson certainly contributed to the show's success, so it was only right that they be rewarded for it.

THE SHAME OF ACTING

For a period in 1995 Duchovny carried in his wallet a photo that he had torn out of *The New Yorker*. It was a Richard Avedon portrait of Tennessee Williams and it showed the face of a man who had lived and suffered but had never given up. Duchovny thought that he would never want Avedon to take *his* picture, because it would reveal too much of what Duchovny had hidden beneath the smooth and handsome face. "I don't think I could handle being captured so truthfully."

An actor who didn't want to be captured by one of the great photographers of our time. Who was afraid of being seen for himself. In the same manner he never felt comfortable when someone he knew, Perrey Reeves or his mother, visited the set and watched him act. He didn't like to drop his guard around such people and so found himself stuttering over his lines. "I guess that stems from shame," he said.

David Duchovny was an actor who was ashamed to act.

Naturally this repression of emotion came out in his acting style, even if it was misinterpreted by critics as underplaying. Duchovny himself has admitted his faults as an actor, that he is inexpressive at times, withdrawn and reserved. As the writer Scott Cohen wrote in *Details*, Duchovny the actor is "like a sleepwalker stuck between morning and night." Ironically, Duchovny was attracted to acting precisely because it could help to let go of some of this repression, to become passionate without the repercussions of real life. It was the old mind/body problem, a kind of unfinished war between his intellectual and analytical side and his physical, emotional one.

Relating to this problem and its effect on his acting is Duchovny's vanity. If there is one thing that literature teaches, from Ecclesiastes' *Vanitas vanitatum* to Thackery's *Vanity Fair,* it is that admiration of the self and of the physical soon falls to dust. Yet Duchovny was a handsome young man and he knew it. Not only that but his career as an actor depended on it; no wonder he had won so many roles where he had to take off his clothes and fall into bed with a woman. Possibly he used this physical charm in real life too, as most good-looking people learn to do from the earliest age, in order to make everyone like them, to seduce (as Billy admits in *New Year's Day*) both women and men, one with the kiss and the other without. But on the other hand, the work ethic and respect for knowledge that his mother inculcated in him, and even his years as a literature student, told him that this vanity was an evil. He felt this but he couldn't escape it.

There is also another way of looking at this question of vanity, one that relates to the existential (and zen) question of knowing the self and being at peace with it. Duchovny, who had always been a self-absorbed and introspective person, scrutinized his inner life and feelings. But once a person becomes concerned or self-conscious about his outward appearance and its effect on others, he moves away from the inner life; instead, he feels 'outside' of himself, observing his own body, objectifying it. It is the actor's dilemma (if part of his art) to know that others are watching him, projecting onto him their own fantasies. He may feel like a mere body, belonging to everyone but himself.

The result of this vanity — or rather Duchovny's guilt over it — was shame. In a revealing moment during an interview published on the internet, Duchovny said: "I'm ashamed of acting as a profession.... It's an exploitative biz. You are depending on charisma. You count on the way you look, the way you sound, to make money. That's the first real level of shame. The deeper level of shame is a real deep shame about selling one's emotional life to others.

It's horrible, like emotional prostitution." This was an extraordinarily strong statement and revealed the intense feeling behind it. That Duchovny could compare his new profession to prostitution showed the depth of guilt and shame that he felt. Many, perhaps even most, actors have no difficulty with drawing on their emotional life for the roles they play; only someone who found emotions as private as Duchovny did would feel this way. One wonders if he is a natural actor, the sort who thrives on attention, exposure, self-display. For him it really is more like therapy, apparently necessary but at the same time deeply painful.

Even more remarkable, however, was the manner in which Duchovny turned this sense of shame to his advantage as an actor. Much in the same way that he made his repressed nature into an acting style, so he found that he could draw on shame. Indeed, it may be shame which viewers see and sympathise with in those sad eyes of his. In another statement he made what adds up to a kind of acting manifesto for Duchovny: "The best actors convey the idea that they never truly get there. The viewer senses failure and disappointment from them. I love when you can smell failure in an actor's performance, because acting is really about displaying yourself for money and for people you don't know. There is a great cost to your personal life. With Brando, for example, I always feel he's showing me that it's painful, certainly humiliating, maybe even wrong and bad to act. The best actors have an air of failure even at the height of their success."

It seems unlikely that Laurence Olivier or Anthony Hopkins would say that it is wrong to act, a humiliation.

British actors tend to have a more objective, professional approach to their craft. Americans — especially those who have studied the method — tend to be more emotional and personal. Duchovny, though, seemed to go even farther than most American actors in his feelings of self-exploitation. It was also true that while British actors often start young, attending one of the prestigious acting schools in London, Duchovny had begun less than ten years before. He was really still a new actor, raw and unformed, trying to work out his ideas and feelings. Being famous, however, would not make things any easier.

ELEVEN

THE THIRD SEASON

A cult show no longer, *The X-Files* was an unqualified hit. It even earned itself a comic-book parody in *Mad Magazine* (called "The Ecch-Files"). Chris Carter said it was because people wanted to be frightened and mystified, that Americans had "a sort of New Age yearning for an alternate reality" combined with a deep suspicion that the government routinely lied to them. He added, "Either that, or the Fox network has an *amazing* marketing department."

Along with the general praise, however, came criticism that the show's anti-government paranoia helped to foster the sort of fanaticism that resulted in the bombing of a government building in Oklahoma City. Duchovny was sceptical of such a connection. "I think the show is simply of our time," he said. "I don't believe that art creates what happens in life. They are definitely connected, just not causally." (His expression of the idea that two things could be connected without one causing the other proved that his analytical powers certainly returned to him when he wasn't acting.) As for the question of whether the show should be censored, he responded by noting that the political impulse to suppress artists has existed since Socrates wanted to ban poets from the Republic. And he quoted Yeats on how the dark stories of our time will inevitably be told: "A terrible beauty is born."

The second season had ended with an old-fashioned cliff-hanger; was Mulder, trapped in a buried and burning boxcar, actually dead? The previous episode, "Anasazi," continued with the second-season opener, "The Blessing Way," in which Mulder was saved and healed by a group of Navaho indians. Hard at work again after the hiatus, Duchovny found himself moody and introspective. When he had signed that pilot contract so long ago he never thought that he would still be playing the role of Fox Mulder. He couldn't help imagining all the different roles he would like to play but couldn't, even as he realized that every life, even an actor's, has its definitions. "You have to deal with the depression that your life is not limitless, that you won't play every role," he said in an attempt at resignation.

Given the difficulty of living in two different countries, not to mention Duchovny's extreme reluctance to commit himself in a relationship, it was not surprising that his romance with Perrey Reeves finally ended. As a celebrity romance it could not end merely with a kiss goodbye; instead, both actors' management issued press releases announcing the break up. Not long after, Duchovny was spotted going out with Kristin Davis, the actress on *Melrose Place*. About relationships he said, "This business is hard because you're constantly around new and exciting people. . . . And also you're constantly being stroked. You're wonderful, you could have anything you want. And eventually you go, 'Damn, I deserve it.' "

And Duchovny, despite his misgivings, could not help falling into the life of a celebrity. For one thing, the network expected him to do his share of promotion for the show. For another, it is difficult for any mortal to resist the temptation of being the object of so much favourable attention. Duchovny did hundreds of interviews and though he always felt reluctant at the same time he found himself enjoying the process, perhaps because his self-absorbed nature made it interesting to think about himself and the roller-coaster life he was now living. Part of the problem, he admitted, was that he had not developed a protective shell, that fake surface that can make a celebrity seem callous or just plain phoney. Duchovny found it hard *not* to be honest. "Bits of myself leak away, are given away," he sighed. "And that's less for me and my loved ones to have." Just as he did not want to be photographed by Avedon, he found that more superficial talk shows and interviews were easier to take than an in-depth conversation with someone like Tom Snyder. Joking with Leno or Letterman there was much less danger of giving away any of his real self. However, even in the most casual newspaper interview he sometimes mentally wandered, free associated, or couldn't help intellectually seducing the interviewer. He might drift on about how sexual dolphins were or suddenly announce that he'd like to be the first person to in a television commercial to actually demonstrate the use of toilet paper. He often came off as both outrageous and emotionally needy.

By the end of the show's second season Duchovny's celebrity still felt novel and he was trying to work through his own feelings about it. "The adoration part doesn't register as adoration," he said. "Sometimes it registers as pressure. But, I don't know, it's fairly new to me. I'm just trying to feel my way through it. I'm new to the celebrity thing. So I'm trying to figure out how I can live a happy life and also not alienate people who have good wishes for me."

One thing he definitely didn't like was being pointed at in the street. For one thing, he felt that he was famous just for being famous in that typical American fashion, not for having done anything heroic or memorable. Television, Duchovny believed, tended to flatten out events and people, making everyone a celebrity on the same level regardless of achievement. Also, he didn't like the fact that he could no longer observe other people in a restaurant or a park now that *he* was the object of *their* scrutiny. And he positively hated people associating him personally with the character he played. When people shouted at him in the street, he thought at first that there must be some movie star walking behind him. Later, after hearing the umpteenth person call out "Hey, Mulder!"

he wanted to shout back, "I'm not fucking Mulder, you know?"

Asked by Rosie O'Donnell about how he feels about his fans, Duchovny told a story about "the weirdest letter I got that was actually an erotic poem cut up like a jigsaw puzzle. I had 'enis' and I had to find the letter that went with it but all I had was an 'h.' So I ended up with 'I want your henis.' I also had a 'gina' and I was looking for something else and I got the state of 'Virginia.' That poem didn't turn out as it was intended."

Considering Duchovny's nature it follows that instead of merely basking in the limelight it should make him more thoughtful. He brooded on the public's image of him and their apparent concern over whether or not he was a "nice guy." Why should it matter? As long as he was a good actor he was doing his job, but the public always seemed to want more. They thought he had some sort of power whereas he didn't feel as if he had any at all. And because he was good at one thing he was supposed to have gained some larger moral insight. He recounted how at a premier for *Batman* (getting invited to such events in order to add to their glamor was a typical celebrity role) a reporter asked him who made his suit (Armani) and what he thought of the Clinton health care plan. Banality and significance seemed to merge into absurdity.

"The trouble with celebrity is that people equate it with meaning," Duchovny decided. Meaningless or not, though, he was stuck with stardom and he seemed genuinely mournful about his loss of anonymity. As he noted, a star could never have a normal life back even if his career failed at some point. Then he would be a has-been and a running joke.

Of course stardom had its good points. For one thing, there was the money. Duchovny had watched his mother have to go to work to support him and his brother and sister, which was one reason she had urged him to excel at school. Now he was making more money than he knew what to do with, although not as much as a lot of basketball stars or the bigger film actors. And as Duchovny pointed out, his agent took 20 percent and the government 40, leaving him with less than people thought. He compared it to Hemingway's *The Old Man and the Sea* — all the little sharks eating away the big fish until there is almost nothing left.

Money wasn't the only reward of stardom, however. Duchovny was invited onto *The Late Show with David Letterman*, which felt like an "exercise in surrealism" to him because he had watched the show for so many years. Even here he felt the pressure, not to be honest so much as to make the audience laugh. *The Tonight Show* did not ignore him either. He took advantage of his good looks (no matter how much shame he felt) to be a model for the Saks Fifth Avenue Fall 1995 designer catalog. He played basketball against some pros on MTV's *Rock & Jock*. And in what had to have been the most trivial use of the knowledge gained in his academic career, he appeared on *Celebrity Jeopardy!* Duchovny was beaten by Stephen King, a popular writer maybe but no intellectual slouch.

And then came *Saturday Night Live*. Despite the show's long and slow deterioration (almost nobody thought it was funny anymore), the live program still attracted hip, young viewers who often tuned in to see the celebrity guest. Being a guest host was one of the recognized marks of stardom. Duchovny joined the cast for a week of nerve-wracking rehearsals in preparation for the last show of the 1995 season, during which he felt sure the show would never pull together. He played basketball with the writers in a deliberate attempt to win them over. On the night of the live broadcast both his brother Daniel and his sister Laurie came to sit in the audience. (During the program Duchovny would manage to motion to his sister from the wings, showing by a scissor-motion of his fingers that he liked her new haircut.)

The show opened with a taped *X-Files* take-off in which various regulars on *Saturday Night Live* claimed that they had been attacked by a "beast man." Acting like Agent Mulder (and giving the regulars orders as if they were Scully), Duchovny went after the beast man only to discover that he was another regular, Chris Farley, stealing everybody's lunch.

Then came the first commercial break, while Duchovny waited nervously behind the stage-set door, ready to come out on cue for his monologue. He appeared, dressed in a three-piece gray suit, to wild applause and proceeded to make fun of his movie career which had not yet seen him appear in a hit. "Oh yeah," he added, "I'm also on *The X-Files*. That's just to pay the rent until *New Year's Day 2*."

The skits that followed ranged in quality from the passable to the execrable — about the usual quality for the show these days. Duchovny appeared as a dumb biker type in a game show called "You Think You're Better Than Me?" and, in homage to *Twin Peaks*, as a

woman in wig, dress, and stockings. (He allowed himself to be more playfully feminine this time.) Next
came a quick appearance as Robin the Boy Wonder,
followed by a talk show in which he played a Richard
Gere impersonator. Whether he was supposed to be
angry, confused, or disgusted, Duchovny played Gere
with the same expression of slight distaste — a silent
joke on the occasional complaints about his own inexpressive style. Overall, Duchovny did not embarrass
himself, but neither did he fare as well as those actors
whose large and manic presence can fill the void left
by the absence of a good script.

Afterwards producer Lorne Michaels held a party
at the Rockefeller Plaza skating rink and the celebrities came out in droves. Kevin Nealon, one of *SNL*'s
long-time regulars, locked Duchovny into a friendly
full-nelson hold. Crowded among the glitterati of
New York, Duchovny failed to look happy.

He had more fun performing on *The Larry Sanders
Show*, calling it his favourite comedy on television. The
HBO show attracted a small but cerebral audience
with its mock talk-show format, its cynicism and
sharp humor. Duchovny asked to play himself as a jerk
and the writers were happy to oblige. Getting his time
on the show squeezed to only a couple of minutes,
he told Sanders off backstage and then pleaded to be
asked on again. By playing an egomaniac, Duchovny
was sending up what he called "the infantilization of
actors" — stars acting like children, taking tantrums
and making selfish demands. It was a way of warning
himself not to lose perspective.

In all these appearances Duchovny was testing his own celebrity, trying to discover why he was both attracted to and repelled by the life of stardom. Perhaps he had, like Faust, made a pact with the devil, but even so there were some things he refused to do. First and foremost among them was his rejection of invitations to appear at *X-Files* conventions. Put on by Creation Entertainment, the same company that has turned such a good profit with *Star Trek* conventions, they began with one in San Diego in June 1995 that was attended by 2,500 people. There and at the others that have followed fans of the show have been able to meet Chris Carter as well as Gillian Anderson and other stars, who have been paid in the neighborhood of $15,000 for their presence. (The fans also get to buy t-shirts, videos, comic-book versions, and other paraphernalia.) But while Duchovny would likely be the biggest draw, he has resisted meeting so many of his admirers face to face, especially since these are the people who most closely identify him with the character of Fox Mulder. Along with his instinctive dislike of the idea of appearing so that fans can idolize him, he knew that it would only further his connection to the role and make his chance of a career after *The X-Files* more difficult.

INTO THE FOURTH SEASON

The success of *The X-Files* meant even more attention on its stars and creator for the fourth season. Would Chris Carter continue to keep the show fresh and original? Fans and critics debated its direction. Edward Gross, a writer for *Cinescape* magazine, published a long analysis of the show in the summer before the fourth season in which he argued that the government paranoia theme had overwhelmed other aspects of the show to its detriment. (Carter, however, did not agree.) Another question was whether Carter would maintain the same high personal level of involvement in the show, especially as he was preparing a new series for Fox called *Millennium* which would take over *The X-Files'* Friday time period as that show moved to Sundays when it would have a chance to gain a larger viewing audience.

For some time there had been talk of an *X-Files* movie which would give Carter an opportunity for an even more complex story line, a much larger budget for special effects, and the opportunity to make a lot of money. Finally in May 1996 Carter got around to working on a script. Duchovny's feelings about playing Mulder in a movie were mixed to say the least. At first he simply denied any interest, saying that it would tie him to the character even more. But later he had to admit that the idea of someone else playing *his* role was not very pleasing either.

Duchovny had been longing to get back to feature-film acting and had finally found enough time to sign on for a non-Mulder role. He would play a mafia doctor in a movie called *Playing God*. He was also harboring ambitions to direct, although so far he did not yet feel ready for the challenge. But in one of his sexual similes, he compared film directing to sex; no matter how much you read about it you can only learn by doing. He hadn't given up the idea of writing either, but he no longer seemed sure that writing was what he was meant to do either. "I'm not totally satisfied just acting," he said. "I think my life will be a series of attempts at things. I've given up thinking I've found the one thing that will satisfy me."

During the summer of 1996 Duchovny took some time out to help promote the show. On the same day that he was scheduled to appear on Letterman he was

a guest on Rosie O'Donnell's new morning talk show.
O'Donnell seemed in overdrive that day, mugging, singing, talking to the audience — doing anything she could think of to hold their interest. In contrast to her hyperactivity, when Duchovny slouched onto the show he seemed almost anaemic in his reserve and low energy. His jaw needed a shave, his combed-back hair looked wet as if he had just stepped out of the shower, and his tired eyes did not seem to want to open.

Nevertheless, or perhaps because of his dishevelled look, he looked handsome and even romantic. And it was clear he wanted the audience to like him even while at the same time he gave off an air of disdain. He talked about some fan letters he was receiving in the form of erotic jigsaw puzzles (this was an old story, but he made it funny anyway). He spoke of the long and tiring shoots and the monotony of playing the same character. O'Donnell asked if he really wrote poetry and whether or not it rhymed, revealing her impressive lack of knowledge of contemporary literature. Duchovny replied by saying his poems were "garbage." He meant that because he wrote them on napkins and bits of paper he was always losing them or throwing them out, but in a strange way he also seemed to be deliberately insulting his own writing, telling himself that it had no value.

When O'Donnell asked Duchovny about the problems of fame, he admitted to using false names for registering at hotels, such as Onesto Stubbs, Felix Bumperhumper, Coco Marx, and Moishe Miller (the latter made up of his paternal grandfather's first name and his mother's maiden name). And then he spoke in that slightly tremulous, even pained way of his about being a celebrity.

"It's flattering and it's wonderful but it can get a little scary at times. [The fans] want so much from you in a strange way," he said. When they told him how much they liked him he didn't know how to reciprocate, what to offer them that would have any real value. "So actually what I do," Duchovny went on, suddenly hardening his voice, "is say, 'Why don't you get the hell out of my face.' "

The audience laughed. Duchovny gave a slight smile, his eyes still only slits as if he could not bear the lights. He was learning to get the audience to love him even while he told them to get lost.

He was, at last, becoming a real celebrity.

INTRODUCTION: "David Duchovny" by Leslie Tucker, *Us* June 1992. **CHAPTER ONE:** "David Duchovny" by Eirik Knutzen, Copley News Service; "Looking For Space Aliens (and Denying Yale)" by Maureen Dowd, *New York Times* March 26, 1995; appearance on *The Late Show with David Letterman*, aired April 1996, transcript from the internet; "Going To X-tremes" by Michael A. Lipton, *People* April 25, 1994; "X-Files Undercover" by David Wild, *Rolling Stone* May 16, 1996; "The X-Man" by Scott Cohen, *Details* October 1995; *Book Review Digest* 1970; appearances on *The Tonight Show*, transcript from the internet; "Making Contact with David Duchovny" by Jenny Higgons, *Playgirl* April 1995; "Secret Agent Man" by Steve Pond, *Us* June 1995; Brian Lowry, *The Truth Is Out There; The Official Guide to The X-Files* HarperCollins 1995; Los Angeles Associated Press. **CHAPTER TWO:** Higgons; Lipton; Lowry; "You're Not Going To Try To Take a Shower with Me, Are You?" *Entertainment Weekly* from the internet; David Duchovny, *The Schizophrenic Critique of Pure Reason In Beckett's Early Novels* (Princeton B.A. thesis) 1982; Dowd; "Devil's Advocate" by Marc Shapiro, *Starlog* May 1994; "David Duchovny" by Malissa Thompson, *Seventeen* December 1995; Pond; Knutzen; "David Duchovny: The X-Files Star Who's Out There" by Scott Williams, Associated Press January 19, 1995; Cohen. **CHAPTER THREE:** Dowd; Cohen; Lipton;

Knutzen; Williams; "Gillian & Dave's X-cellent Adventure" *TV Guide* March 11, 1995; "X-Symbol" by Julianne Lee, *Starlog* May 1994; Thompson; Los Angeles A.P.; "Movies" by Bruce Williamson, *Playboy* 1989; Lowry; Tucker; Lee; Pond; "X-Files Dossier: David Duchovny," *The X-Files Magazine* Winter 1996; "X-Factor Actor" by Jack Hitt, *Playboy* Nov. 1995; *Tom Snyder*; "Coffee, Tea, and David Duchovny" by Rhonda Krafchin, *Pyrdonian Renegade* from the internet; "The X-Files Dossiers," *TV Zone* May 1996; *People* Feb. 10, 1986. **CHAPTER FOUR:** Pond; Lowry; Lee; *The X-Files Magazine*; Krafchin; Cohen; "The X-Files" by James Martin, *America* Oct. 21, 1995; Los Angeles A.P.; Knutzen; Thompson; appearance on *Rosie O'Donnell*, aired July 18, 1996. *Spectrum* July 1995; Leonard Maltin, *Leonard Maltin's Movie and Video Guide 1995* Signet 1994; Higgons; "Movies" by Bruce Williamson, *Playboy* 1991; Hitt; "Movies" by Bruce Williamson, *Playboy* 1991; "Religion Taken To the Breaking Point" by Janet Maslin, *New York Times* Sept. 30, 1991; "The Rapture," *Variety*. **CHAPTER FIVE:** Maltin; "A Genuine X-centric," *Entertainment Weekly* Dec. 2, 1994; "Paradise Lust" by Michael A. Lipton and Sue Carswell, *People* June 15, 1992; Lowry; Dowd; Los Angeles A.P.; Wild; Cohen; Higgons; Shapiro. **CHAPTER SIX:** Higgons; Wild; "A Private Conversation with Chris Carter," interview on video release of "Pilot/Deep Throat" episodes; *Entertainment Weekly*; "Gillian & Dave's X-cellent Adventure" by Deborah Starr Seibel, *TV Guide* March 11, 1995; Lowry; Dowd; Shapiro; Knutzen; "X-Files Hunk Can't Stay Faithful," *Australian Women's Day* Oct. 9, 1995; *The Tonight Show*; Radio Times interview (British Broadcasting Company) from the internet. **CHAPTER SEVEN:** Dowd; "A Genuine X-centric"; Shapiro; Thompson; Williams; Cohen; *Spectrum* July 1995; Lowry; Krafchin; *Radio Times* interview; *TV Zone*; Seibel. **CHAPTER EIGHT:** Lowry; Shapiro; "X-Files Uncovered: An Interview with David Duchovny," *Rolling Stone 1995 Rock & Roll Yearbook* (Australia), from the internet; *Tom Synder*; Krafchin; Thompson; *The Tonight Show*; Los Angeles A.P.; *Radio Times*; Lipton; Dowd; "You're Not Going To Try To Take a Shower with Me, Are You?"; Hitt; Cohen; Seibel; "Hollywords" by Philip Jackman, *Globe and Mail* August 1, 1996; internet sites; "David Duchovny," *Entertainment Weekly*, from the internet; Lee; "Big Time: X-Files Star David Duchovny Looks For Praise in All the Wrong Places" by David Perry, *Cinescape* #7, 1995; Knutzen; Williams. **CHAPTER NINE:** Krafchin; Thompson; *Rolling Stone 1995 Rock & Roll Yearbook*; Cohen; Anderson; Dowd; Higgons; *The Late Show with David Letterman*; *The Tonight Show*; Hitt; Lowry; "You're Not Going To Try To Take a Shower with Me, Are You?"; Williams; Lee. **CHAPTER TEN:** Seibel; Lowry; Martin; Higgons; Anderson; Lee; *TV Zone*; Cohen; Hitt. **CHAPTER ELEVEN:** Lee; *Tom Snyder*; Cohen; Lowry; Higgons; "David Duchovny," *Entertainment Weekly*; *The Tonight Show*; *Rolling Stone 1995 Rock & Roll Yearbook*; Anderson; Wild; internet sites; Hitt. **CONCLUSION:** "David Duchovny," *Entertainment Weekly*; Dowd; Hitt; Lee; Wild; *TV Zone*; *Cinescape* August 1996; *Rosie O'Donnell*.

DUCHOVNY AND SUZANNE LANZA

DUCHOVNY AND PERREY REEVES

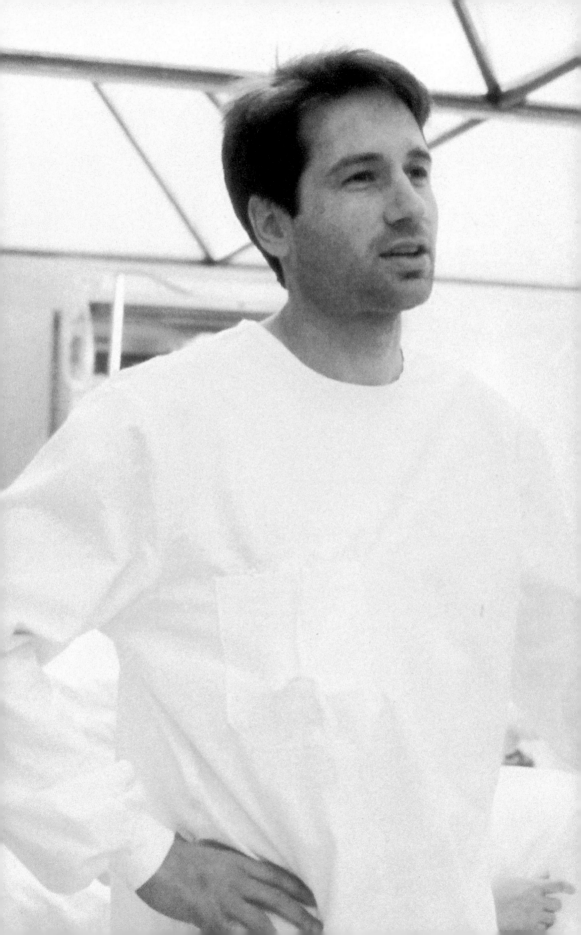

CHRIS CARTER AND DUCHOVNY

DAVID DUCHOVNY'S APPEARANCE ON THE LATE LATE SHOW WITH TOM SNYDER, JULY 7, 1995

TS: David Duchovny stars in one of the most talked about TV programs, *The X-Files*, Friday night on Fox. It was called a cult hit, but when it won a Golden Globe Award for best drama, the cult favorite became a mainstream hit. Before you [*referring to Duchovny*] came on here, we got nine pages from people who follow *The X-Files* on the internet. We have the David Duchovny Estrogen Brigade, reports on David

Duchovny's pets, restaurant habits, personal life, clothes, everything. Do you follow what goes on on the internet?

DD: I'm the main supplier of information for those people, obviously. I follow some of it. They send me flowers, if they know where I am going, and things like that. I'm just flattered by the whole thing. I don't know the intricacies of the information and things like that.

TS: But have you gone on-line with these people?

DD: I did it once, very quickly, but it was kind of like going into a room and everyone saying hello at once, and that was the depth of the conversation. It was just "Hi David," "Hi David," "Hi David," and then I had to go and and it was like, "Bye David," "Bye David," "Bye David." So that it ended up in the fact sheet, of course, that David like to say "Hi" and "Bye."

TS: But there were no in-depth questions about how you crafted the character of Mulder or how the show came to be?

DD: No, thank goodness because there was not much crafting done.

TS: I have not seen you on too many interviews like this. Do you avoid it as a matter of course or is it just that it has not come up?

DD: No, I have done a few talk shows, but no shows where I could sit and have a conversation. There is part of me that would avoid it because you know there is something scary about revealing too much about yourself in a situation like this.

TS: How so?

DD: I think on a talk show you are entertainment, meant to be a funny person. They expect that, that is the entertainment. You don't actually have to give of yourself. You don't have to give and take in a conversation with another human being. It is a more frightening proposition [to do this].

TS: Let me ask you about what *The X-Files* will do to the rest of TV. How many shows of the 1995–96 season will try to emulate what you did because of the show's great word of mouth and success?

DD: Right, right. I think that some people's jobs are to follow trends and try to capitalize on them. However, I do not think there is a science fiction trend or anything like that. I think *The X-Files* is a good show and you have to make a good show to duplicate it. Just by making a show science fiction is not going to duplicate it.

TS: No. But if they try to replicate it and don't do it as well, does it lessen the quality of what you have done?

DD: No. It's like, "Is The Rutles less than The Beatles?", not that we're The Beatles, but it's flattering. Hopefully, it will make us seem that much better. Maybe they'll say that such shows are faux *X-Files* or whatever.

TS: I know you pursued your education with diligence, majoring in English and working toward getting a Ph.D. I have wondered with actors who pursued education with diligence, how much of it do you have to set aside to be an actor? Acting is really feeling not thinking, isn't it?

DD: Right. It's more instinctual. In fact, it was odd when I first tried to become an actor. I was almost at a disadvantage because of the many layers of analytical or critical thinking that I had to throw away. All these muscles that I developed were devalued and made me a more boring actor more than anything else. The most boring acting is intellectual, you know? The most exciting acting is instinctual. In terms of breaking down scripts and story arcs and things like that, however, my education helped, but not in terms of the heart.

TS: But before you stumbled into acting, if that is what you did, what were you pursuing in English? What was your goal?

DD: I wanted to write. I was getting a Ph.D. because I guess I did not have the guts to do it on my own. I was going to be in an academic environment, read the best books, write about them, and maybe on my spare time do some of my own writing. So that was the plan. Stay in academia and eventually start to write.

TS: What happened?

DD: I don't know. Well, I was at Yale and so I saw all those acting students all the time and they seemed to be having a great time. I wanted to write for stage or screen and I thought I should find out what kind of dialogue fits, so I started taking acting. My heart was not involved in what I was doing. The further along that you get, if your heart is not involved, the harder it is to stay. If you have the fortune to get out, you should, and I did.

TS: With the series in Canada and your rigorous schedule 14 hours a day, was it a surprise to you? People not in film think you have it made. They think that you say a few lines and then go home.

DD: It was very surprising to me. The problem is that no one wants to hear you complain if you are on a TV show. I can sit here and say it's hard.

TS: What is the hardest part?

DD: The hardest part is combining the workman, punching in for 14 hours a day part, with the creative, artistic side. No one says to a painter, "You have to paint 14 hours a day, ten months of the year" because a painter would be scribbling stick figures. The problem for me is to not do the acting equivalent of stick figures. It's hard because you get empty. You are there every day and don't get a chance to rejuvenate. There are days when I go home and know I didn't do well, but I have to forgive myself because I know I am human.

TS: We are going to the phones now.

Caller Theresa from New Haven, Missouri.

TS: Hello.

CALLER: I was wondering if you have any movies coming up or if you plan on doing any?

DD: I would love to, but the hiatus was only 7–8 weeks, so it was not possible to do a movie. Next year I hope to do one. Nothing for me except *The X-Files* for the next little while.

TS: Well, remember that you do something for cable called the *Red Shoe Diaries*. He has a full plate now.

DD: Yes. There is an extensive video collection of my work, but you'd have to find a really good video store to find the kind of low budget things that I've done.

CALLER: I have some. *Baby Snatcher.*

DD: Hold on. That's enough. You don't want to get into it.

TS: *Baby Snatcher?*

DD: It was just a side deal.

TS: What was the title?

CALLER: *Baby Snatcher.*

DD: Don't make her say it four times.

TS: If she does, she wins the car. (*Pause*) The thrill of hosting *Saturday Night Live*. Wow.

DD: Yeah. There was nothing like it. The whole week before I basically didn't eat. Because I thought it would not come together. You don't think it will come together. There's nothing there until 9:30 when you are putting together the final show. You think you will be nervous, but you realize that your entire human energy is focused on the show.

TS: What about when they announce your name?

DD: You are back there behind the door and you are testing the knobs to make sure that they will open. It's just pure. You just get filled up. It's an amazing feeling.

TS: Do they want you to be funny?

DD: Yeah, they kind of write for you or to you. It helps if you are funny. That is kind of what the show is about. It's kind of like being with your relatives, "Do you do any imitations, Dave? Do you do anything funny? Do you do animals? Celebrity impersonations? Do you dance? You can't? We'll write something for you. We'll make it work. Can you stand there and look mildly funny?"

TS: Were you pleased?

DD: Yes, I was very pleased. I thought the show was pretty good and I was really proud of it. I had a great time.

TS: After they had the party?

DD: Yeah.

TS: With the drinks and stuff?

DD: Yeah. It was the last party of the year.

Caller Jason from Milwaukee, Wisconsin.

CALLER: Do you have the same beliefs as Mulder?

DD: Not necessarily. Certainly not as passionately. I

am more of a "show me" person. I'd believe in UFOS
or aliens if they landed on my head, but that is about
as far as it would go.

CALLER: Does Gillian Anderson believe what Mulder
believes in real life so that it is kind of vice versa of
your characters?

DD: I think she is more open to it. Actually, we are
identical to our characters and for people to believe
we are good actors, we created this hoax that we are
the opposite of our characters.

TS: We have a clip of the show.

[*Short clip of Fox Mulder and Dana Scully in the forest with
umbrellas. Frogs appear to fall out of the sky onto them.*]

TS: The *Red Shoe Diaries* appears on cable. You are on
it?

DD: Yeah, right.

TS: It's a character who is bewildered about what
makes women the way they are?

DD: Yes.

TS: It's been described as soft romance?

DD: Yes. Soft-core pornography.

TS: What happens in *Red Shoe Diaries?*

DD: In the pilot, my fiancée kills herself and I find her
diary. In it she chronicles an affair she had and I am
baffled. In the end, I take out an ad. I ask people with
secrets they can't tell to anyone, to tell them to me,
the lonely guy with the dog.

TS: [*Laughing*] Heather in Fort Nelson, B.C. Hello
. . .

DD: Oh, that's where we shoot.

[*Some confusion on the line as caller tries to ask her question.*]

TS: Heather, your question please?

CALLER: Um, I would like to know if *The X-Files* shows are based on real FBI cases?

DD: I don't think so. That's all I can say. It's based on stories the writers make up. I'm sure they go off stories in the paper that they can fictionalize, but they are not based on real cases, as far as I know. It would be a hell of a lot easier to write, if they were.

TS: Sure would. There would be a lot more of them. Bye Heather.

DD: Bye.

TS: We put Heather out of her misery. [*Laughs*] On *Twin Peaks*, you had the transvestite part. Did you enjoy that role?

DD: Yes. It was a lot of fun. It's not often that you get to wear a bra, panties, and a dress, and get paid for it.

TS: I know. [*Laughs*] Did you have to be shaved?

DD: [*Laughs*] Yes, I shaved from my mid-thigh down. It was funny because at the time I swam to stay in shape. I would go to the gym and shower. I'm sure the guys thought, "Who's the guy in the fur shorts?"

TS: [*Laughing*] I guess it's been a while since the beer commercial.

DD: Yep. Yep. I can't say anything more.

TS: You don't need to. I have enjoyed this more than I can tell you. Thank you for your time. I especially thank you for your good sense of humor.

DD: You're welcome. My pleasure.

INTERVIEW WITH DAVID DUCHOVNY

by Diane Anderson

Not only is Vancouver cold and rainy, Studio 5 happens to be filled with 110 tons of imported snow kept cold by $200,000 of refrigeration. Such a spectacle is unheard of for a day of television shooting. But this is more than television: it's the creation of a Friday night ritual where viewers partake in the scary and the sacrosanct. After accolades such as a Golden Globe award, *The X-Files* family deserves to indulge. An extravagant Arctic set surely seems worth it. Today [January 31, 1995] they are shooting and wrapping

"End Game" written by Frank Spotnitz which airs February 17 and finishes the story started in "The Colony," which David Duchovny helped think up. Like Mulder, Duchovny is attached and detached in equal parts, but his voice fluctuates slightly more than the monotone character he plays on TV. I met him and his dog Blue in Vancouver, B.C., where the show is filmed.

FOX MULDER VS. DAVID DUCHOVNY

DAVID DUCHOVNY: Describe myself in three words? David William Duchovny. William is my mother's father's name. My father used to sing a song, It Ain't Necessarily So: "Little David was small but oh my! He slew big Goliath who lay down and lieth." But my father claims I'm named after the statue of David. Um. That was his favorite sculpture and so that's who I'm named after. A statue. And I've tried to pattern my acting style on that as well.

DIANE ANDERSON: And you've been pretty successful at being a stoned face actor so far?

DD: [*Laughs*] Uh, I don't know.

DA: Does Duchovny really mean ghostly or spiritual in Russian?

DD: A Hungarian said it means confessor or secret lover. I like all three.

DA: Describe Mulder.

DD: See, that's a tough question because y'know I play him in the show. I think other people would describe him better. I guess we have a lot of similar qualities. To me, Mulder's got attachment and detachment in equal parts. That's how I try to play him. He can be totally detached and off in his own world and then suddenly attached and passionate about something — those are his constantly cyclical moods.

DA: You see that in yourself?

DD: Yeah, definitely in my own kind of fake Zen approach to life which is passionate detachment. That's my own fake Buddhism.

DA: Do you practise Buddhism?

DD: Not really. It's fake because I don't really practise it. It's just this philosophical thing I try to do. I try to keep in mind that everything is meaningless — but yet that's not a very happy place to live. From there, you can either say, "Life is meaningless, why do anything?" Or you can go, "Everything is meaningless and therefore every little thing has any meaning you wanna give it." Wallace Stevens would be my mentor in this. I place the jar in Tennessee and there's no reason for me to place it there except that I'm doing it in the moment.

DA: So you are the Emperor of Ice Cream?

DD: Exactly. Let be be the finale of seem. Right? Stevens is great. I like Ashberry too although sometimes there's not enough like confession and sex in his poems. Sometimes I want more dirt. Although I respect poets for creating really powerful poetry without having it resort to any kind of personality which is kind of amazing — some poems have no charisma. It takes a lot of integrity when you think about it in this day and age where everything is sold on charisma and hype and things like that. So as a matter of fact,

I'm going to backtrack and say that I love the fact that there's no sex or personality in them.

ON TECHNOLOGY

DA: So you bailed on your Ph.D. — a.b.d [all but dissertation]. When did you decide to act?

DD: You ask that like you'd ask a serial killer, "When did you first think you wanted to kill people?" Like, "When did you decide to inflict this misery upon the world, David?" [*Laughs*] When I was 27 or 26. I was in grad school. My sister is in NYU graduate school. She's getting her Master's in Education, but she also teaches so it's going to be a long process.

DA: It is a long process, but you were almost at the Ph.D. finish line.

DD: [*Laughs*] I thought Yale was always ashamed of me. But I wrote some good papers there.

DA: What would you have done your dissertation on?

DD: It was gonna be on magic and technology in contemporary American fiction and poetry.

DA: Go on.

DD: Can I just tell you something? Usually when I say that NOBODY asks a follow-up question. You're the first one who has said, "So what?" 'Cause no other reporters want to go there with me. Nobody wants to go there with me.

DA: Do I not want to go there with you?

DD: No, yeah, yeah go there. Um. See, I don't have very far to go there because all I had was a topic. I never really finished . . . so basically here's my spiel — I thought it was a good one and it probably would've made a good dissertation. I read a review of Christopher Lasch by Richard Rorty in the *New Yorker*. Culture of Narcissism. Rorty attributed some things to Lasch that would've fit well in my paper which would've gone something like this: I was looking at technology as a sphere of knowledge that had no moral codes built in to it. Meaning that if you can do it technologically, you do it. If you can build a bomb, you build a bomb. Nobody says, "Let's not build a bomb." I guess there have been movies made about certain voices who have said, "Maybe we shouldn't make this bomb," but in the end if technology has been there, mankind has made it. Humans never say "No" to the technology. Do you know what I'm saying?

Magic on the other hand is a primitive technology that has many codes built into it. There's black magic, there's white magic. A lot of moral codes are built in to magic. Therefore, I was looking at writers who were discussing technology in terms of a magical field and trying to infuse it with morality in that sense. So I had Mailer's *Of a Fire on the Moon*, and things running throughout all his work. Pynchon's *Gravity's Rainbow*, and *V* and James Merrill who wrote "Changing Light at Sandover" and all these poems on an ouija board. And Ishmael Reed who's a very militant opponent of what he says is white technology as opposed to, like, African humanistic magical power. That was going to be it. I don't know how it would've played out. Y'know how it is when you write a paper — you have a big idea then play it out specifically, it totally changes. So that was the big lie of the idea. And it would've played out as something else. I don't know what.

DA: What do you think of technology and moral codes?

DD: I don't think there's a possibility. It's like Faustus. If you can do, you do it. It's too tempting. I don't think people have the willpower not to use the technology they have. I mean, who's not going to use a toaster? You gotta use it. It's there; you want burnt bread; you put it in the toaster.

DA: Is that good or bad?

DD: I couldn't say good or bad. It seems like an inevitable thing, but I think it's too bad. It'll probably end up hurting a lot of us. It seems we've come to an age where I guess the whole dream of technology was going to free people. Marx even wanted it to do that. It was supposed to give us more time and make our lives easier. But people seem to work as hard as ever even though we have all these machines, and so I don't see it ever getting to a point where technology is going to make our spiritual lives easier. It's made us more comfortable physically, but I don't know how wonderful a thing that is because I think a certain amount of physical suffering is good. I think that's why everybody goes to work out now 'cause they miss physical suffering. We don't — unless we have a physical job — we don't get to use our bodies. We don't get to feel that wonderful pain of actually being animals working with our bodies. We go to the gyms like rats and mice. It's the same as it ever was. Everyone has always been afraid and alienated. That is *la condición humane*. Despite all these machines, we seem to have less and less time which doesn't make sense to me. I think people are more alienated because they don't do people-to-people work anymore, it's phone-to-phone, fax-to-fax. That is pretty alienating. I had a conversation in L.A., once I had a 6-hour day on the phone. I went through all these different emotions and I realized I had just gone through the entire range of human emotions holding a piece of plastic to my head. I wasn't actually in the presence of anybody. I think people have always distrusted the government — as we should. I think people like the show because it's smart and scary and it's a good ride. I don't think it's a zeitgeist kind of a deal, like so many reporters are claiming.

ON WRITING

DA: You wrote your undergrad thesis on Samuel Beckett and here you are filming an episode called "The Colony."

DD: The show was kinda my idea. I had an idea and I told it to Chris, and he said, "That kinda jives with an idea I've been playing with and let's see if they hang."

DA: Did they hang?

DD: They hung. They hung well. They were well-hung. So we'll see if it works out. It woulda been more exciting if I woulda had time to actually write some of it. I just don't have time — period. To write you need to concentrate and you need time. That's what Chris does. He has a really hard job — he writes and produces — he's got his finger everywhere. It woulda been scary because I act like I'm a really good writer. I'll be disrespectful of certain scripts and stories and then I'd have to put up or shut up so that would've been kinda scary for me.

So luckily all I had to do was have an idea, I didn't have to write anything.

DA: Would you ever want to write an episode?

DD: I'm not sure I'd want to write one of these. So much of my life is doing this show that the last thing I would want to do is write one. I would like to write something else — something, something, Something. The outside of a toothpaste tube, something, anything, a cereal box. I would like to write the Colgate copy. I don't know, I have a couple ideas that I've had for a few years that I'd like to write, but again that would be a fearful enterprise to embark upon because I really think that I'm a good writer and then to actually face the fact that I may not be. I don't know if I wanna face that yet. That's what I truly think is my natural ability. Like I said, as an actor I have these stumbling blocks. Inexpressiveness. Withdrawn. Reserved. In writing I have the opposite fault. I'm like totally mandarin; I overwrite. Mandarin. That's what Charles Berger (he was my advisor) said. I wrote a novel in grad school — an attempt at a novel — and he said the writing style was "mandarin" and I always remember that. And now I like mandarin collars. So I'm mandarin. I'm inclusive — everything and anything I think of is in there to express and there's no narrative line. As an actor I'm much more critical of narrative line and editing — take this out, I wanna see it make sense and see it go there. In writing I throw everything in. I wrote a novel about someone very similar to me. A bartender. In New York. At The Continental. It was like *Bright Lights, Big City* — or very similar. I wrote in the third person with the same drug-induced, sex, self-conscious, mid-80s, Bret Easton Ellis — need I go on? But it was okay. There was some good writing and very good chapter titles. I really loved my chapter titles.

DA: What was the best one?

DD: "The Spider and the Fly." It was about a dream the character had where everytime he tried to pull down his fly, a spider would come down. The character had to urinate in the dream and he couldn't because every time he tried to pull down his fly, the spider would come down so I just thought that was funny, the spider and the fly.

DA: Are you afraid of spiders?

DD: No. I don't love them, but I'm not afraid of them. I don't like to walk my face through cobwebs because you don't know if the spider fell down your collar. But I think the book came from a dream I had.

I'm not in danger of wetting my bed very often. Your subconsciousness edits you. So in my dream, something in my brain sent the spider to prevent me from peeing in my bed. I thought that was interesting — that, even in the dream world, the superego, or whatever you want to call society's restrictions, is powerful enough to prevent you from going.

DA: Was *The Spider and the Fly* the name of your novel?

DD: No, it was called *Wherever There Are Two.* People ask Jesus about the new church, "How do we know when there is a church?" He says, "Wherever there are two gathered in my name, that's a church." Communication is the important thing. In a splintered family unit, two people making a connection was enough. I guess the book is autobiographical, but I wouldn't want to go into it. . . .

[Speaking of flies, for you DDEBers who ponder end-lessly the boxer vs. briefs query, I can attest to having seen a pair of black (or were they grey?) Calvin Klein boxer-briefs in DD's scattered trailer. That isn't to say it's a religious practice or even his preference. After all, he did don that horrid Speedo in some episode or another.]

ANXIETY OF INFLUENCE

DA: What are your influences?

DD: Music. If I'm doing a scene that I want to have a certain flavor or movement for, I think about the music I want for that. Sometimes music, sometimes painting. . . . I have a photograph in my bag right now that's been influencing me. This is a photo I've been working with. [Pulls out a page ripped from a *New Yorker*, a photo of Tennessee Williams taken by Richard Avedon.] Things like this influence me a lot. I look at this face — I saw such combo of pain and will to keep going so amazing. It made me vow I'd never let Richard Avedon take my picture because he sees too much. I don't think I could handle being captured so truthfully.

DA: Are you guarded?

DD: You have to pick your spots. Who would want to be consumed on a mass basis as who they were? It just doesn't seem like a nice thing to me. I would try to be as truthful as I can to people close to me. One of the things about acting that's probably the most fun is that you get to be truthful in a really dishonest way. I mean you are most truthful when you tell the truth as a lie. It doesn't have to be right, just has to be true.

DD: Film and TV acting are different, not in kind. Just in time.

DA: What is your favorite role or when did you feel most truthful?

DD: My projects are all children to me and I wouldn't want to play favorites.

DA: One anthem of the show is Trust No One. If you had to choose someone to trust, yourself and your dog not included, who would it be?

DD: My older brother comes to mind. I'll just have to go with it. He does *Red Shoe Diaries* wraparounds. I admire his focus. Working with a sibling is interesting. It's different to be demonstrative in front of family members. Or like my girlfriend [Perrey Reeves] was in the vampire episode? It's weird, I'm more giving in my work than in life. And my mom came up to Vancouver. She was on the set and I found myself nervous, stuttering. I totally choked on a light scene. I lost my voice. I guess that stems from shame.

DA: Tell me about the shame.

DD: I'm ashamed of acting as a profession. My mom never — well, she does now that I'm doing okay — but she used to not approve of my choice, giving up academia for acting. It's an exploitative biz. You are depending on charisma. You count on the way you look, the way you sound, to make money. That's the first level of shame. The deeper level of shame is a real deep shame about selling one's emotional life to others for money. It's horrible, like emotional prostitution. I see a pain in Brando when he exposes himself. He has trouble opening up. I think the greatest actors have that. I hate it when actors are all over the place and give the audience cues for when and how they are supposed to react. That's when I feel like a big fat liar. Like, "Okay, I am going to cry now so you, the audience, should know to feel sad. If I err it's on the side of withdrawing too much. In the episode "One Breath," perhaps the most emotional show, Mulder is raging and had to cry once. I chose to cry in a place other than where it was written. Mulder doesn't cry in the presence of the person cried for [Scully], he cries when he is alone. Ashberry said that the art part is what's left out. I try to include the clues instead of painting by numbers and spelling it out — that's when I feel like a shithead.

ACTING BENEFITS

DD: The flip side is that it is the greatest job in the world. Things that are prohibited in real life, you can do as an actor. What you keep yourself from doing in real life — because of law or love or concern for another person — is totally okay on camera. I get to fire my gun, I get to blow somebody's head off, I get to beat up the lover of my wife, I can fuck this girl, I can fuck this guy if I want to. You get to do all those things as an actor and there are no repercussions.

IDENTITY CRISIS

DA: Do you ever feel like your individuality is being eclipsed by character you're playing?
DD: Yeah, it's a scary feeling. I get a little resentful at times 'cause people yell "Hey Mulder!" It's like,

"Fuck you, I'm not Mulder; it's a job I do." I'll get over it. It's an infantile thing I'm going thru right now. My manager sometimes accuses me of taking work home. "Oh, you're acting so much like Mulder." And maybe I do. I don't think of myself as that kind of an actor, but maybe I am.

DA: Do you ever find yourself discovering parts of your personality? What Mulder trait would you like to have?

DD: Yeah I do see parts of myself in Mulder. But Mulder doesn't care what other people think of him — that's his total strength. Mulder's total strength is Not Caring. The ultimate freedom is not giving a shit.

DA: And you do?

DD: Oh yeah! I have to care what others think of me. It's my business y'know. Again in my fake Zen religion, I hope to move to a place where I don't care, but that's a journey. I'm not there yet. That may be my ultimate goal. That's the ultimate freedom — not to give a shit about what anybody else thinks.

B-BALL

DA: Let's talk about basketball — can you slam?

DD: No.

DA: How tall are you?

DD: Six feet. I mean it's possible that a 6-foot man could dunk, but not this 6-foot man. I was just thinking about Melville for a second. [*Pause*] In *Moby Dick*, there's a description of cutting up the whale — the overlong description.

DA: Which one?

DD: It talks about a whale's penis being 6 feet. So sometimes I think of myself as a whale's penis 'cause I'm 6 feet. Sometimes I refer to myself as a whale penis. It's conceivable that a whale penis could dunk, but not this whale penis. Hey — can you have that be the first line of your story? Duchovny likes to think of himself as a whale's penis?

DA: You tell me. Can I?

DD: Yes! I'd be disappointed if you didn't use a quote like that.

DA: Do you like the Knicks?

DD: Do I like the Knicks? I love them. I would die for the Knicks. I would throw myself in front of a train for John Starks any day. I played on MTV *Rock & Jock*. I played with Chris Webber.

DA: Did you?

DD: He's good. But I really like Cliff Robinson. That was weird cause his persona on the court always seemed to me kinda babyish. But in person he was a cool, cool guy. And Reggie Miller who I hated 'cause he almost beat the Knicks. So Reggie Miller . . . I kinda hate him 'cause he's loud and he dissed Spike. I didn't think he had that much personality and I thought the media was creating him because there was no Michael left and NO LARRY no Magic . . . so let's create Reggie. Shaq — we don't know what Shaq is yet, he's an amazing player and he has a rap album but — so Reggie Miller was gonna be another one [media creation] so I hated him. He was sitting down on the bench and as usual, I hate people in abstract but when I'm in their presence I'm in love with them so I see Reggie Miller and I'm thinking, "It's fuckin' Reggie Miller" so I go up to him and say, "Hi, I'm David Duchovny, Reggie. It's nice to meet you." And he goes, "Oh, I know who you are! I watch your show all the time!" and now I'm really in love with him.

So we're walking off the court at the end of the game and I'm almost to the locker room and I feel this tap and I turn around and it's Reggie and he goes, "Can I get a picture of you? My sister's in the stands and can I get picture with you?" And now I'm totally in love with Reggie and I go, "Now it's gonna be hard to hate you in the playoffs next year." And he goes, "Please don't hate me." Me and Reggie! I came up to his armpit. He's skinny but he's tall. Really skinny. The other thing is I should've traded jackets because my mother's maiden name is Miller so if I play — because we all got these warmups with our names on them, mine had Duchovny and his had Miller — so next year if I play I'm gonna ask him if we can trade.

TELECOMMUNITY

DA: Do you want to get that [ringing phone]?
DD: Nah. I have people call just so that you think I'm important. So it's actually not even anybody that needs to talk to me. Like a character from a Congreve play who likes to make himself seem important who will often leave messages for himself, and he'll send a carriage for himself with him as a driver and, not finding himself at home, sometimes sit and wait for himself. I can't remember. I just like the idea of him calling on himself and not finding himself home will wait for himself so that's what I'm doing. Is any of this interesting? I need to know if I'm a big crashing bore.

DD: I'm in the bathtub; the water's running, I'm trying to heat it up. I got the day off. I take baths whenever I get the chance. In fact, wish I had a mobile tub to carry around with me. Reporters ask me if I had always wanted to be an actor and the truth is when I was 4 or 5 my dad asked me what I wanted to be and I said a bathtub. I can't remember why. I wish I was that kid that thought that up. My dad's explanation was I had all these plastic dinosaurs that I loved — I was a complete archeologist freak and I knew all the names. When I took a bath I would dump all the plastic dinosaurs in with me. I'd fight tyrannosaurus rex against triceratops. Whoever was spoiling for a fight that day would have it. My dad thinks that by being a bathtub I would ensure never having to be without my dinosaurs. I like his explanation; it's simple and draws everything together. As an actor, when someone asks, "Could you play a rastafarian priest?" I think I just don't have it in me to stretch like that. Then I remember I was going to be a bathtub — that's about the farthest stretch I've heard anybody do so I think yeah I could do that.

DA: What have you learned about money?

DD: You make a lot of money as an actor but you lose a lot of money. It's like someone is trying to throw you a pass but there are like three defenders intercepting the ball and the ironic thing is you hire these defenders who take a chunk out of the ball. They work for me. I don't spend a lot of money so I assume I'm saving a lot of money. But seeing someone's salary printed in the paper is an illusion. An agent and a manager, that's 20% right there, you give 40% to taxes. It takes a while before you get any money. It's like *The Old Man and the Sea*. By the time you reel the big fish in it's been eaten away at by little sharks. An actor's salary is a carcass on the beach — a big shark-eaten tuna.

DA: The character you play Fox Mulder logs in with the computer password TRSTNO1.

DD: I wouldn't even know how to log in. Although, I am getting a computer soon. Our producer Chris Carter is so fed up with me not having a computer he is going to buy me one and I'll pay him back. A Powerbook.

DA: So, if you get a computer, what'll be on your hard drive?

DD: I don't even know what that means. I guess I'll put something hard on it. I can't even engage in that conversation because I don't know anything about computers.

DA: Your show is popular with nerds and netheads. There is an *Internet for Dummies* book in your trailer. You must have some interest in communication technologies.

DD: The DDEB [David Duchovny Estrogen Brigade] sent me that book. I haven't even cracked it. Communication is an overrated thing. I can communicate just fine with the tools I have. I don't have to talk to anybody I don't know.

DA: I heard Delphi put you and your co-star Gillian Anderson online?

DD: I think it was a very atypical adventure because they were all so like excited and disbelieving that it was actually me. "Are you really David?" and "Hi! Hi! Hi!" I think if I went on again and spent more time it'd be different.

DA: You wouldn't have to go as yourself.

DD: Anytime you start looking for information about yourself not as yourself you are asking for trouble.

DA: What is the most reliable source for your info about the world?

DD: My five senses. Is that how many I have? My six senses.

DA: Now, as Fox Mulder you find yourself involved in all kinds of covert government activity. Conspiracy abounds on *The X-Files*. What do you think of today's political scene?

DD: I think people have always distrusted the government as they should. *The X-Files* would've done well after Watergate. The current political climate with all these bozos out there? It's hard to believe that any of them are competent enough to perform a wonderful cover-up like we attribute to them. Idiots in office are hurting the success of *The X-Files*. I'd prefer to have smarter people in office to help our show. I see people like Orrin Hatch and I wonder, How did this guy graduate high school?

DA: If you had to make fun of somebody who would it be?

DD: Someone who needs to come down. Newt Gingrich, maybe.

DA: There are New Twit posters all over the Bay Area. What do you think of him?

DD: New Twit. That's good! He seems to be a fool, a nincompoop. But I'm glad that he's in a position of power because he will fail miserably and never get further than where he is. I'm glad he's where he can't destroy the country but only injure it. People are already seeing what he is. Newt's a knucklehead. I think if Newt were more competent our show would be in the top ten. America would believe that politicians could be hiding information if only our leaders were more intelligent.

DA: What do you think is most evil about him?

DD: His sincerity problem and his own self-belief.

DA: Are those the most dangerous things for anybody?

DD: Absolutely. Newt's out to get government back on track . . . Ha! He really believes he can save people.

DA: Do you think anybody can save another person?

DD: Absolutely not. The saviors of the world have said that it is within you. He's saying, "Oh here it is — it's in my manual." From the man who wrote science fiction books. Christ, Buddha, all the great teachers have said I can give you guidelines but the experience of faith and truth is very personal and very difficult.

DA: How do you explain the success of the show?

DD: I think people like our show because it's smart and scary and it's a good ride. It tries to do its science homework. It's the first show to try to be realistic in the face of unrealistic or surrealistic things.

DA: The technique of the show is offering patterns of images presenting people as bewildered beings in an incomprehensible universe. It's what Martin Esslin might call Theater of the Absurd.

DD: Yeah, *Twin Peaks* was tongue in cheek and took the most mundane things and made them surreal. We take the most surreal things and make them mundane or possible. We got there first, we filled a hole, and now there are a bunch of other shows like *Sliders* and *VR-5* following. We are the trace blocker; we are in the keyhole. Hollywood tries to make recipes for success and I'm not sure that is the best strategy. I was in a 19th Century Literature class and the professor was talking about specialization of the body? He told us the armpit didn't really exist before deodorant. That is what has happened with the show. "Oh my god there is a need *The X-Files* is filling, the need is probably bigger than the show. We should make other shows like it." Chris Carter's brilliant move is to take the it seriously and as a possible source of poetry. He doesn't talk down to it but treats it as a legitimate source of human endeavor, this paranormal stuff. People who wouldn't normally like sci-fi crap like the show because it doesn't approach it in a kooky way. The truth is out there. OUT THERE — as in far-out. Or it is out there to be found. My take is more, The truth is in there. I think the truth is within us. But, how many shows promise the truth? C'mon let's go find it. Friday Night at 9:00! A human person is never happy; he is always searching for more. Religions offer faith. People who have true faith are blessed and profoundly happy.

DA: What did your father believe in?

DD: My father believed in words. And taught us to appreciate them through jokes. My father is Jewish and since I don't read or speak Hebrew, my father would spell out prayers phonetically for me if I had to do one for Seder or something. But I didn't practise a religion. I think life has any meaning you give it. The Buddha says I have eternal life [that's a *Caddyshack* reference, by the way] so I have that going for me.

DA: If, for some strange reason, you don't have eternal life, what would you like to be remembered for?
DD: My particularly individual b.o. If you write a book or movie, people always can hold onto that work. I want to be remembered for something evanescent.
DA: What's the strangest part of being famous?
DD: The other day this guy comes up to me and asks if he can buy me a drink and I said, "No, just give me the 5 bucks."
DA: No you didn't.
DD: You're right. But I'm gonna start.

DAVID DUCHOVNY FILMOGRAPHY

Working Girl (1988)

PRODUCER: Douglas Wick

DIRECTOR: Mike Nichols

SCREENPLAY: Kevin Wade

CAST: Harrison Ford, Sigourney Weaver, Melanie Griffith, Alec Baldwin, Joan Cusak, Philip Bosco, Nora Dunn, Oliver Platt, James Lally, Kevin Spacey

Working Girl is the rags-to-riches story of Tess McGill's (played by Melanie Griffith) rise in the financial world. She impersonates her boss (Sigourney Weaver) and jumps to the head of the queue. David Duchovny plays a bit part as an old friend of Tess who attends a birthday party for her in the old, blue-collar neighborhood.

New Year's Day (1989)

PRODUCER: Judith Wolinsky

DIRECTOR: Henry Jaglom

SCREENPLAY: Henry Jaglom

CAST: Maggie Jakobson, Gwen Welles,
   Melanie Winter, Henry Jaglom, Milos Forman

Drew (Henry Jaglom) arrives in Manhattan on New Year's Day to discover the three women who were the previous tenants have not yet vacated. The women — Lucy (Maggie Jakobson), Annie (Gwen Welles), and Winona (Melanie Winter) — invite Drew to stay with them for a party. David Duchovny plays Billy, Lucy's jerk boyfriend who is the reason she is leaving New York. After Billy hits on three different women, he sleeps with Lucy's roommate, Annie. Seeing them, Lucy throws him naked out of the apartment. Interestingly, Maggie Jakobson was David Duchovny's real-life ex-girlfriend.

Bad Influence (1990)

PRODUCER: Steve Tisch

DIRECTOR: Curtis Hanson

SCREENPLAY: David Koepp

CAST: Rob Lowe, James Spader, Lisa Zane,
   Tony Maggio, Marcia Cross, Christian Clemenson

As the title suggests, this is the story of friendship and corruption. Aspiring yuppie Michael Bol (James Spader) meets and befriends handsome Alex (Rob Lowe). Alex turns out to be highly corrupt; this attracts Michael at first, but soon he is led too far over the edge by the murderous Alex. David Duchovy plays a small role as a clubgoer in a bar frequented by Michael and Alex.

Duchovny and Henry Jaglom in *New Year's Day*.

Twin Peaks (1989–91)

PRODUCERS: David Lynch, Mark Frost

DIRECTOR: David Lynch

WRITERS: David Lynch, Mark Frost

CAST: Kyle MacLauchlan, Michael Ontkean,
  Madchen Amick, Dana Ashbrook

In David Lynch's "eerie, erotic" TV series, Duchovny appears in the second year as Dennis/Denise Bryson, the transvestite detective. Rosie O'Donnell kids Duchovny that he appeared more lady-like in *Twin Peaks*, especially by wagging his head back and forth to fan his wig. Duchovny responded that "I decided when I was doing the character that women are allowed in society to be more open and expressive than men."

The Rapture (1991)

PRODUCERS: Nick Wechsler, Nancy Tenenbaum,
  Karen Koch

DIRECTOR: Michael Tolkin

SCREENPLAY: Michael Tolkin

CAST: Mimi Rogers, Patrick Bauchau,
  Kimberly Cullum, Will Patton, Terri Hanauer,
  Dick Anthony Williams

Bored telephone operator Sharon (Mimi Rogers) indulges in small-scale orgies with her boyfriend Vic (Patrick Bauchau) and various strangers. Sharon turns to God and transforms a swinging friend of hers, Randy (David Duchovny), into a Christian. They marry and have a daughter. Randy is shot

A hot scene from *The Rapture*, with Mimi
Rogers, Stephanie Menuez, and Duchovny.

Duchovny starring as ''Bruce'' in
Don't Tell Mom the Babysitter's Dead.

and killed resulting in Sharon's depression and eventual loss of faith.

Julia Has Two Lovers (1991)

PRODUCERS: C.H. Lehenhof, Randall Davis

DIRECTOR: Bashar Shbib

SCREENPLAY: Bashar Shbib

CAST: Daphna Kastner, David Charles, Tim Ray, Clare Bancroft, Martin Donovan, Anita Olanick

While children's writer Julia (Daphna Kastner) is thinking over a marriage proposal from Jack (David Charles) she receives a phone call from Daniel (David Duchovny). He says he has the wrong number but the two begin a long conversation that eventually becomes a sexual relationship. Julia finds out that Daniel is not what he seems — he is really a sicko who calls women as if he has a wrong number and seduces them. She confronts him but he tells her he has truly fallen for her. Jack leaves Julia and she tells Daniel she needs some time to organize her life. "Duchovny seems to be playing the same guy he played in *New Year's Day*, the kind of man who's good-looking and knows it but who is not so assured beneath the glibness after all" (Kevin Thomas, *Los Angeles Times*).

Don't Tell Mom the Babysitter's Dead (1991)

PRODUCERS: Robert Newmyer, Brian Reilly, Jeffrey Silver

DIRECTOR: Stephen Herek

SCREENPLAY: Neil Landau, Tara Ison

Duchovny and Daphna Kastner
in *Julia Has Two Lovers*.

CAST: Christina Applegate, Joanna Cassidy, John Getz, Josh Charles, Keith Coogan, Concetta Tomei, Kimmy Robertson, Jayne Brook

A teen wish-fulfilment comedy about five kids who are left alone while Mom's on vacation and the babysitter dies. Oldest daughter, Sue Ellen (Suell) Crandell (Christina Applegate), lands a dream job in the fashion industry. David Duchovny plays Bruce, an employee in the same company. Eventually he reveals Sue Ellen as a fraud but she is so popular with clients and skilled at fashion that all is forgiven.

Denial (1991)

PRODUCER: Melanie Green

DIRECTOR: Erin Dignam

SCREENPLAY: Peter Nelson

CAST: Robin Wright, Jason Patric, Rae Dawn Chong

A free-spirited young woman, having had a chance encounter with her ex-boyfriend, becomes consumed by his memory. "Flashbacks," says Leonard Maltin, "are virtually indistinguishable from the present-day narrative."

Baby Snatcher (1992)
(made for TV)

PRODUCER: Carl Dunn Trussell

DIRECTOR: Joyce Chopra

WRITER: Susan Rhinehart

CAST: Veronica Hamel, Nancy McKeon, Michael Madsen, Penny Fuller, John Evans, Roger Bearde

A chilling TV thriller about just what the title suggests. A woman, Bianca (Veronica Hamel), steals a baby from Karen (Nancy McKeon) in order to keep her husband Cal (Michael Madsen) from leaving her. Karen becomes independent and strong from her struggle to find her baby. David Duchovny plays David, the successful, self-absorbed businessman who has a long-running affair with Karen but is not about to leave his wife for her.

Beethoven (1992)

PRODUCER: Joe Medjuck, Michael C. Gross

DIRECTOR: Brian Levant

SCREENPLAY: Edmond Dantes, Amy Holden Jones

CAST: Charles Grodin, Bonnie Hunt,
Dean Jones, Nicholle Tom, Christopher Castile,
Sarah Rose Karr, Oliver Platt, Stanley Tucci,
Patricia Heaton, Laurel Cronin

A comedy about a family who adopts a Saint Bernard named Beethoven who grows to an enormous size and trashes their house. Although the father (Charles Grodin) is eternally complaining about Beethoven, he and the family come to their pooch's rescue when he is kidnapped by evil veterinarian Dr. Varnick (Dean Jones). David Duchovny plays Brad, a priggish snob-evil-yuppie-type.

Chaplin (1992)

PRODUCERS: Richard Attenborough, Mario Kassar

DIRECTOR: Richard Attenborough

Duchovny, Robert Downey Jr.,
and Dan Ackroyd in *Chaplin*.

Brigitte Bako with Duchovny in a dramatic scene
from the erotic Showtime feature *Red Shoe Diaries*.

SCREENPLAY: William Boyd, Bryan Forbes,
    William Goldman

CAST: Robert Downey, Jr., Geraldine Chaplin,
    Hugh Downer, Nicholas Gatt, Bill Paterson,
    Anthony Bowles

The interesting and complex life of Hollywood's greatest funnyman, Charlie Chaplin (Robert Downey, Jr.), is the subject of this Richard Attenborough flick. David Duchovny plays the role of Rollie Totheroh, longtime friend and cameraman to Chaplin.

Red Shoe Diaries (1992)

PRODUCERS: David Saunders and Rafael Eisenman
DIRECTOR: Zalman King
WRITERS: Patricia Knop and Zalman King
CAST: Brigitte Bako, Billy Wirth, Bridge Ryan

"This film," says *Variety*, "is all form and no content, with the gloss of a commercial for an overly ambitious hair spray." David Duchovny stars in the pilot episode of this series as Jake, a successful city planner and architect who discovers his fiancée's secret diaries after her death. The series continues with Duchovny as narrator, making only occasional guest appearances.

Ruby (1992)

PRODUCERS: Sigurjon Sighvatsson, Steve Golin
DIRECTOR: John Mackenzie
SCREENPLAY: Stephen Davis

CAST: Danny Aiello, Sherilyn Fenn, Frank Orsatti, Jeffrey Nordling, Jane Hamilton, Maurice Bernard, Joe Viterelli, Robert S. Telford, John Roselius, Lou Eppolito, J. Marvin Campbell, Richard Sarafian

The story of Jack Ruby, the man who killed Lee Harvey Oswald. Ruby (Danny Aiello) is portrayed as a smalltime crook, in over his head with the mob. He shoots Oswald to reveal the real presidential assassination plot. Instead he is jailed, never able to tell his story. David Duchovny plays a small part as Officer Tippit.

Venice / Venice (1992)

PRODUCER: Judith Wolinsky

DIRECTOR: Henry Jaglom

SCREENPLAY: Henry Jaglom

CAST: Nelly Alard, Henry Jaglom, Suzanne Bertish, Melissa Leo, Daphna Kastner, Diane Salinger, Zack Norman, Marshall Barer, John Landis

American independent filmmaker Dean (Henry Jaglom) goes to the Venice Film Festival in Italy where he meets and gets romantic with French journalist Jeanne (Nelly Alard). While attempting to cast roles for his next movie, Dean films various women who speak directly and revealingly into the camera about life and love. David Duchovny plays Dylan.

Kalifornia (1993)

PRODUCERS: Steve Golin, Sigurjon Sighvatsson, Aristides McGarry

Brad Pitt, Juliette Lewis, Michelle Forbes
and Duchovny driving in *Kalifornia*.

DIRECTOR: Domenic Sena

SCREENPLAY: Tim Metcalfe

CAST: Brad Pitt, Juliette Lewis, Michelle Forbes, Sierra Pecheur, Gregory Mars Martin

Brian Kessler (David Duchovny), writing a book about famous serial killings, decides to travel to California with his girlfriend Carrie Laughlin (Michelle Forbes), stopping at the famous murder sites along the way. They pick up a white-trash couple (also a real-life couple, at the time), Early Grayce (Brad Pitt) and Adele Corners (Juliette Lewis), to help pay for gas. Early turns out to be a killer and winds up taking Brian and Carrie on a murderous rampage before Brian can finally bring him down. Duchovny's eyes, says Ira Robbins in *Newsday*, "have the same expressionless animal quality as Richard Gere's."

Playing God (1997)

Duchovny plays a down-on-his-luck doctor who has lost his licence because of a drug problem. Also stars Timothy Hutton. "I didn't know how those guys on *ER* and *Chicago Hope* did it," says Duchovny. "But now I know *I* can cut people open. Let's see *them* fight aliens."

SUE'S CANDID MOVIE REVIEWS

I'm a vidiot; I will not rest until I have everything on my own tapes, collecting our hero's past lives on video is a passion. So for you, the curious:

SUE'S MOVIE REVIEWS WITH A SPECIAL "JENIFER KINK-O-METER"

NEW YEAR'S DAY: One of those New York school yack fest movies. DD plays the pathetic boyfriend who hits on three of his girlfriend's guests then sleeps with her roommate. Total nude scene as she throws him out of the apt. without his clothes on. Side view from the knees up . . .

JULIA HAS TWO LOVERS: A very sweet romantic love story. DD plays a guy who calls women on the phone and seduces them. He and she actually fall for each other. DD is very young, cute and TAN. If you like goofy romance, it's a must see.

THE RAPTURE: VERY kinky DD is very hunky with long hair and super buff. Do you want to see him doing two women at once? Do you want to watch him give a hand job to Mimi Rogers (under the covers)? Are you interested in serious religious topics? Do you want to see DD get shot in the chest? Then this movie is for you. (I taped only the parts with him in it and avoided the rest.)

RED SHOE DIARIES: The story of an impeccably dressed rich man (DD) and his psychotic child fiancée. This movie was, umm, Fluffy BUT it has a definitely sexy (somewhat homoerotic) basketball scene that is beautifully photographed. I've never seen DD look so good!

RED SHOE DIARIES 4 — "AUTO EROTICA": Sexy softcore DD proves once again that he is a great on-screen kisser. I guess it's kinda kinky; I don't recommend watching it with Mom and Dad. It's a hole-up-in-your-room for the evening kinda movie.

KALIFORNIA: DD visits old murder scenes while travelling cross country with serial killer Brad Pitt. NICE voice-overs by DD. Funky sideburns, but cute as usual. Not too kinky, but a bit violent. DD looks great in black silk boxers!

. . . and for the obsessed . . .

BEETHOVEN, CHAPLIN: bit parts, a priggish snob in the first, and the camera man in the second (although he's awfully cute in a hat and knickers).

Don't bother with **WORKING GIRL**, he's almost non-existent and he also appears in **DON'T TELL MOM THE BABY SITTER'S DEAD**, but I can't stomach that.

So there you have it. If you're just as enthusiastic about GA then may I suggest the books-on-tape of her reading **ANNE RICE'S EXIT TO EDEN**. A dopey story but GA's voice . . . wow.

Well, there you have it!

MAD

MAGAZINE

THE
ECCH-
FILES

CH-FILES
There's some slimy creature down there, thrashing about in the sewage! It's big... maybe the size of a human!
A slimy, human-sized creature? Aw, c'mon, what would a lawyer be doing down in a sewer?
We found an alien! We found an alien!
Calm down, Moldy! Not everything in this city is an alien!
Someone's gonna have to go in that sewer and find out what's down there! Skulky?
Gee, my favorite thing, crawling around in raw sewage!
Nuts! It's my favorite thing too! I wanted to crawl around in the raw sewage!
Okay, Moldy, you go!
Oh, boy! Oh, boy! I owe you one, Skulky!
ARTIST: ANGELO TORRES WRITER: DICK DEBARTOLO
Do you have a gun on you, Agent Moldy?
Yes, and thanks for the concern! I always felt the bureau didn't care about me!
We don't! It's wet in the sewer! I don't want your gun to get rusty! It's FBI property! Hand it over!
Moldy, what do you think you're doing?
I am going down the sewer!
We have an open man-hole — with a ladder!
Wow, the bureau has such advanced equip-ment!
Agent Moldy says this country is overrun with aliens, but the government keeps them secret!
Let me tell you about Moldy! While traveling at government expense, he flies coach, and stays at cheap hotels!
Oh, okay, I get it! So he's a weirdo!
45

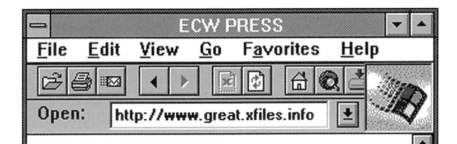

THE
INTERNET
SECTION

INTERNET
DISCUSSION
GROUPS

THE
CHAT
ROOM

The Internet has allowed for the formation of instant discussion groups: *The X-Files*, as a television program, has benefitted from the explosion in Internet access. Viewers can comment directly on episodes of the show, and the actors, minutes after each episode's airing and contribute to an evolving discussion of the extended *X-Files* plotline. Currents of discussion brought up in Usenet newsgroups gradually worked their way outward into print media as coverage of the growing popularity of the program, and the actors, appeared. Internet discussion (and obsession) with *The X-Files* has even been gently lampooned in the series, as Mulder has declined offers from the Lone Gunmen to cruise the net and "netpick" inaccuracies in other television programs. Chat areas serve as forums for all varieties of interest in the show and its principals, from the Duchovny-obsessed to the mythology-obsessed: there's something for everyone to talk about at once.

_____

SUBJECT: **Scully abducted?** Hi, I've just started watching the show and I thought I'd delurk. I know Scully was abducted, but when? In what episode? And what happened? Don't flame me, I'm just a newbie!

SUBJECT: **Re: Scully abducted?** Scully got abducted in "Duane Barry" at the end, or at the beginning of "Ascension," in the second season, and got returned in "One Breath." Those three episodes are GREAT — especially if you're a fan of DD. He does stunts, and is just amazing in "One Breath," especially when he thinks Scully is going to die. After watching a couple of episodes just to get the feel of the show, I'd definitely recommend watching these three.

SUBJECT: **DD is the sexiest man on television (was: Scully abducted?)** How the hell can you mention DD and "Duane Barry" and not mention how HOT he looked in that Speedo coming out of the pool? That man is so sexy, he makes my Fridays. And smart too. That vampire episode "3" is worth watching just for him —

SUBJECT: **Re: DD is the sexiest man on television** "3" was CRAP. What kind of FBI agent would allow a suspect to shave him with a STRAIGHT RAZOR?! The vampire stuff was all wrong, or inconsistent. I guess

Mulder was just too upset over Scully's abduction to be able to think straight. You just can't have a decent X-Files episode without Scully.

SUBJECT: **Best/worst episodes** What are people's favourite episodes? Mine is the Colony/Endgame set — DD helped with the story, and it really did a lot in explaining what Mulder's background is like. We met his father, his mother, maybe his sister — talk about dysfunctional family! No wonder he likes hanging out with Mrs. Scully so much. Mulder will just do anything to find the Truth, and it's amazing to see how far Scully will follow him (and save his ass). Shapeshifters, clones, the alien colonization of Earth, it's The X-Files at its best.

SUBJECT: **X-Files shirts** Does anyone know why the only shirts you can buy with an agent on them have Mulder on them and not Scully? Just wondering. Does anyone have foil-embossed cards from the second series to trade?

SUBJECT: **Anyone ever see Kalifornia?** There's a really interesting scifi cross over in Kalifornia (DD movie before the series started) — Ensign Rho is in it too! Has the X-Files ever used a kind of serial or thrill killer plot — I think I saw an episode with one but I can't remember, the cable went out near the end and I never saw it again.

SUBJECT: **Re: Anyone ever see Kalifornia?** You might be thinking of "Irresistible" (Scully gets stalked by a necrophile) or "Aubrey," the one with the genetically programmed killer. Both are really good, not like the other episodes with the mythology stuff. It's neat to watch Mulder and Scully do regular kinds of FBI work in these episodes. Has anyone read anything by Thomas Harris — he wrote the book Silence of the Lambs. It's

Address: http:\\www.great-xfiles-info

kind of obvious that Scully is like Clarice Starling, but Mulder is a lot like the other FBI agent Harris wrote about, Will Graham in Red Dragon. Graham is a brilliant but erratic profiler who gets into the heads of the killers he pursues, kind of like Mulder (in stuff like "Grotesque" especially). Anyone wonder what Mulder will do once he finally finds his sister? Is that going to be, like, the end of the show and just that? Will he just leave Scully with a case on her hands and walk off into the sunset with Samantha? Or is he looking for something even bigger now?

SUBJECT: **Mulder and Scully and end of series** Whatever they do to end the series, they had better not have Mulder end up with Scully. That would be so cheap. I don't care what the relationshippers say, it's just so OBVIOUS to try to get the two of them together and the X-Files has never been obvious. Sexual tension is good, sex is boring. I mean, not in real life but on tv. Remember how shitty Moonlighting got once they actually had sex? They should never do that to the X-Files.

SUBJECT: **Mulder and the boxcar** How exactly did Mulder get out of the boxcar after Cancer Man had the explosives thrown in it? Did I miss something, or did he just get out between the end of Anasazi and the middle or whatever of The Blessing Way. And did they ever explain what was going on with all those corpses down there? Were they aliens or hybrids or what? I think my cable went out or something since I missed the beginning of the episode anyway. How do you think the new season is going to begin? It's not as much as a big cliffhanger as the last one was.

SUBJECT: **Re: Mulder and the boxcar** Your guess is as good as mine, I think he got out through some compart-

ment but was really injured and that's why the Navajo had to do that ceremony. Yeah, I wonder what they'll do to top that. DD helped with the story on that one didn't he?

SUBJECT: **Re: Mulder and Scully and end of series** SCULLY CAN'T HAVE HIM HE'S MINE!!

SUBJECT: **Worst episodes** I think that episode with the curse and the attacking cats was just plain BAD. How seriously can you take an X-File when it's obvious Mulder and Scully are being attacked by cardboard cats? It's almost as bad as Dr. Who. Or did anyone figure out exactly what was going on in "Hell Money"? Doing those unexplained cases is fine for the agents but what about us? We're supposed to sort of know what's going on.

SUBJECT: **Re: Worst episodes** Even the bad episodes, like that curse of the cat one, aren't absolutely hideous — there's always something to watch. I never feel like I've wasted an hour watching The X-Files. DD can have a good line or two, or GA can look so fed up with the cases, or the setting just looks good. Even the lame ones are worth watching. You never feel like you want that hour back. (I might reconsider that if they ever have Mulder and Scully get together though.)

SUBJECT: **Other work of DD?** What are films that DD has big parts like? All I've seen is Kalifornia, and it was OK, it probably looked really good on a big screen. It was kind of funny that he played an academic guy in it, wasn't it? Is there any way to find out what else he's been in?

SUBJECT: **Locations of cases** Has anyone got a list of the states the cases have been set in? And what states

Address: http:\\www.great-xfiles-info

seem to be the most weird (with the most visits from Mulder and Scully). I'm trying to set up my vacation and I want to know if I'm likely to get abducted or alien tested.

SUBJECT: **Re: Locations of cases** So far it looks like New Jersey may have hosted the most cases (2), but I'm not sure. I know there's only been one foreign case (Dod Kalm, near Norway). If you consider the books and the comics New Mexico wins hands down, but that may just be because of Roswell. How much information is there on the Roswell incident? You read about it a lot but is there a bibliography or a bunch of books out there? There's lots of stuff about how it was just a weather balloon but I know there's got to be more.

THE X-FILES DRINKING GAME

by Matt Schulte

(http://netaccess.on.ca/~bnelson/FBI-XFD/xfls.html)

HERE'S THE DEAL: Every time an event occurs, take the assigned amount of drinks from a beverage of your choice.

I SIP

- Every time Scully is examining internal organs of a corpse.
- Every time Mulder or Scully gets a call on the cellular phone that ISN'T their partner.

Address: http:\\www.great-xfiles-info

- Every time a flashlight that is so bright it requires a car battery is used in a totally dark room.
- If Mulder mentions that something could be paranormal and another character thinks he's joking.
- If Mulder just happens to know some obscure case reference or fact that just happens to be similar to the case that they are working on.
- Any time Mulder decides it would be fun to go into a dark place alone.
- Any time Scully brings up some political/scientific fact.
- Any time when Mulder and Scully split up and Scully goes somewhere on a wild goose chase, so that she missed the whole thing and doesn't believe Mulder when he tells her about it.

2 SIPS

- Every time a mysterious character shows up at the end of an episode to keep Mulder from learning the truth/to save their lives.
- Every time someone knows about Mulder's sister, but won't tell him about it.
- If a computer does something computers don't do.
- If you see the numbers 11/21, which correspond to the birthday of Chris Carter's wife.
- Whenever Mulder is called by his first name.
- Every time Cancer Man lights a cigarette.
- Every time Mulder mentions his sister's abduction.
- Whenever Mulder eats sunflower seeds.

3 SIPS

- Whenever Mulder is called "Spooky Mulder."
- Every time Deep Throat or Mr. X is summoned.
- If M and S get into a fight.

4 SIPS

- If a UFO appears in Scully's presence.
- Whenever someone gets sick during an autopsy.
- If Scully decides it would be fun to go in a dark place alone.

EVENT REQUIRING SPECIAL ACTION

- Mulder and Scully get romantically involved: Drown yourself in your drink.
- The case is completely solved with no unanswered questions and it ends up that the ghost haunting the house is a guy with a mask trying to decrease the property values and Scooby Doo and the gang end up helping out at the end: Same Action.

Address: http:\\www.great-xfiles-info

X MARKS

THE SPOT

A GUIDE TO THE VANCOUVER LOCALES WHERE THE X-FILES IS FILMED

by Laurel Wellman

(http://www.vanmag.com/9408/XMarks.html)

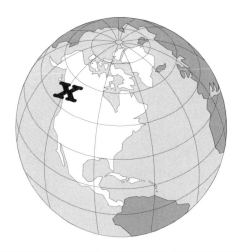

Every week on the cult-television hit show *The X-Files*, special agents Scully and Mulder crisscross the continent in pursuit of UFOs, genetic mutants, and covert government daring-do. But few viewers know that Scully (Gillian Anderson) and Mulder (David Duchovny) never leave a region known as "The Grid." It's hardly Nevada's hush-hush Area 51; rather, it's the geographical zone in the British Columbia Lower Mainland within which film crews will work without travel penalties.

We asked Todd Pittson, one of two *X-Files* location managers, to give us a tour.

L
O
C
A
T
I
O
N
S

---

1. REALITY: **City Square Mall**,
       12th and Cambie
    TELEVISION: **Office building**
       66 Exeter Street, Baltimore

    A mutant makes its papier-mâché and bile nest under one of the mall's escalators in "Tooms." Shoppers may feel queasy riding the escalator after watching the beast get munched in the works.

2. REALITY: **Buntzen Lake**, Port Coquitlam
    TELEVISION: **Lake Okobogee**, Iowa

    B.C. Hydro would probably frown on any UFO caught singeing trees on its property, so the props department created some realistically burned fakes, trucked them in, and set them up in the park for "Conduit."

3. REALITY: **Iona Island Sewage Treatment Plant**
    TELEVISION: **Newark Sewage Plant**,
       New Jersey

L
O
C
A
T
I
O
N
S

Twelve hours of filming here on a sweltering July day were as much as *The X-Files* crew could take. Luckily, Mulder's hunch that a Russian mutant would pop up in a cesspool proved correct.

4. REALITY: **Simon Fraser University**,
   Burnaby, B.C.
   TELEVISION: **FBI Headquarters**,
   Washington, D.C.

Those who've carped about the brutalist architecture of the Arthur Erikson-designed campus must feel the drafty structure has finally received its due. Look for shots of SFU's facade lettered as the J. Edgar Hoover Building.

5. REALITY: **Lighthouse Park**, West Vancouver
   TELEVISION: **Olympic National Forest**,
   Washington State

Mutant (yes, again) insects eat hapless loggers from the inside out, leaving them mere shells in Episode 19, "Darkness Falls." G-men plan a covert spraying program, but just to be safe, don't drink from that tap at the trailhead!

6. REALITY: **Powertech Labs, Inc.**, Surrey
   TELEVISION: **Secret Facility**,
   Mattawa, Washington

After an Iraqi fighter downs a UFO over Turkey, the feds spirit the surviving alien — or "extraterrestrial biological entity" — to Mattawa. Powertech Labs, incidentally, is a B.C. Hydro subsidiary. What do they do? "Some kind of research," shrugs Pittson. *Hmmmm.*

7. REALITY: **Steveston Village**, Richmond
   TELEVISION: **Kenwood**, Tennessee

Having served as Steveston, Maine, home to homicidal transsexual aliens, scant weeks earlier, Steveston is again witness to murder as a faith healer battles the forces of darkness. Even more mysteriously, Coquitlam's Riverview Hospital appears just off the touristy main drag.

8. REALITY: **Versatile Shipyards**,
   North Vancouver
   TELEVISION: **Maryland Waterfront**

Mulder discovers evidence of a human/alien hybridizing project in an abandoned warehouse, but government bad guys whisk it away before he can show anyone.

9. REALITY: **Boundary Bay Airport**, Ladner
   TELEVISION: **Ellens Air Force Base**, Idaho

Despite warnings from Deep Throat, a mysterious informant with CIA ties, Mulder tries to catch the USAF test-flying a secret UFO-based aircraft. And you thought those were just Cessnas . . .

Address: http:\\www.great-xfiles-info

THE
TOP TEN
LISTS

by Lain Hughes

(http://ww2.netdoor.com/~lainh/XFtopten.html)

TOP TEN WAYS OTHER SHOWS ARE RIPPING OFF THE X-FILES

10. Roseanne now claims to be alien abductee.

9. Cast of "Baywatch" actually cloned from leftover parts of Cher.

8. "CBS Evening News" set to replace Connie Chung with a Yeti.

7. Jay Leno says his giant chin is the result of government experiments.

6. "Larry King Live" changing name to "Close Encounters of the Larry Kind."

5. Mysterious next-door neighbor on "Home Improvement" revealed to be Deep Throat.

4. On "Seinfeld," Kramer finds an alien implant in his hair.

3. Principal Skinner relates an out-of-body experience he had in Vietnam on a very special episode of "The Simpsons."

2. Regis will look for aliens while Kathie Lee handles the autopsies.

1. Dr. Niles Crane will start setting fires with the power of his mind.

Address: http:\\www.great-xfiles-info

TOP TEN LINES YOU'LL PROBABLY NEVER HEAR ON *THE X-FILES*

10. "The alien is speaking, Agent Mulder. . . . I think it wants to phone home."

9. "Sure, we could have these people killed to protect what they know . . . but isn't that a little harsh?"

8. "I've seen this one before, Scully. His name is Casper, and he's what we call a 'friendly' ghost."

7. "Look under the mask . . . this is no swamp monster . . . it's Mr. Handy, the owner of the old country store!"

6. "My Lord! This conspiracy involves all three of the Gabor sisters!"

5. "Well, Agent Mulder . . . you caught us. We'll co-operate fully, of course. What would you like to know?"

4. "You'll be happy to hear, Assistant Director Skinner, that I've switched over to the nicotine patch."

3. "The president wants to see you two immediately. His cheeseburger is possessed."

2. "And it would have worked, too, if it hadn't been for you meddling FBI agents!"

1. "Gosh, I guess we were wrong . . . the government did have our best interests at heart, after all!"

THE X-FILES WORD SEARCH PUZZLE

by John R. Potter

(http://www.neosoft.com/~jrpotter/xfiles.gif)

```
L I V E K E C Y R K X E L A M
D A N A S C U L L Y E B O R P
D E E P T H R O A T E M X R O
E S M Y S T E R I O U S E A F
S S N V K I L L E R C N G N U
T M P I Y D O B D N N E E A D
N O E R V U D E E I N D N M E
E K R E O E R I K T U E E N I
M I R P S C L S R G G A T U F
I N A O J A R B M I X T I G I
R G Z R B E C F F U T H C E S
E M I T T I B F X E L U S N S
P A B L T L U C C O I D A O A
X N A I C E G A T S O H E L L
E X P A R A N O R M A L C R C
```

AGENT	CORPSE	HOSTAGE	PROBE
ALEX KRYCEK	DANA SCULLY	KILLER	REPORT
ALIEN	DEATH	LONE GUNMAN	RITUAL
BIZARRE	DEEP THROAT	MR. X	SMOKING MAN
BODY	EVIL	MULDER	UFO
CASE	EXPERIMENTS	MURDER	WALTER SKINNER
CHIEF BLEVINS	FBI	MYSTERIOUS	
CIA	GENETICS	OCCULT	
CLASSIFIED	GUN	PARANORMAL	

File   Edit   View   Go   Favorites   Help

Open: http://www.great.xfiles.info

INTERNET RESOURCES

WORLD WIDE WEB SITES

These should give you an idea of the widespread popularity of The X-Files *and of the actors, as well as neat links to related areas (law enforcement, UFOs, strange science, Vancouver geography . . .)*

http://www.thex-files.com
This is the official Twentieth Century-Fox site for the show.

http://chaos.taylored.com/sites/x-files.html
This is a good place to start to learn about newsgroups and mailing lists dedicated to the show and to Duchovny.

http://www.rutgers/edu/x-files.html
This is one of the first sites dedicated to the show.

http://www.webcom.com/munchkyn/x-files.html
This is the site of one of the keepers of the DDEB FAQ — she also writes the trivia questions for Fox's "X-Test" on their site.

http://www.exit109.com/~fazia/DDEB.html
This is the original DDEB page — where it all began.

http://www.eden.com/~miri
This is the DDEB3 site.

http://www.squidge.org/duchovniks
This is the Duchovniks site.

http://www.neosoft.com/sbanks/xfiles/xfiles.html
Very interesting X-Files site, with links to the FBI homepage, among other things.

http://web20.mindlink.net/a4369/mq.htm
Ever wonder about the places in Vancouver where the X-Files is filmed? This site has the X-Files guide to Vancouver, B.C.

http://cfn.cs.dal.ca/~ae387/X-Files.htm
This Canadian Maritimes site has a lot of interesting links to information about the types of weird, unexplained phenomena featured on the show.

http://www.cs.unibo.it/~cobianch/index.html
Italian site.

http://bundy.hibo.no/~Larsen/x-files/x-files.html
Bilingual Norwegian site.

http://www.stack.urc.tue.nl/~danny/x-files/x-files.html
Dutch site (in English)

http://miage.unice.fr/~mathery/index.html
Unilingual French site, much different than the North American sites.

http://www.ozemail.com.au/~chengmy/xfiles/xf.html
This site is in Singapore.

http://www.geocities.com/Hollywood/4256/
This Malaysian site has links to information on the unexplained.

http://www.cs.mu.oz.au/~simc/xfiles.html
This site is one of many in Australia.

http://www.unix-ag.uni-kl.de/~kleinhen/xfiles/x-files
German fans of the show should look into this for info on German-language mailing lists and newsgroups.

http://wwwdzp.pp.se/x-files
Swedish-language site.

THE X-FILES IN-JOKES LIST

by Laura Witte

(http://www.nashville.com/~subterfuge/xfiljoke.html)

This is my attempt at compiling a list of the inside-jokes from *The X-Files*. I cannot take credit for recognizing many of them. While I did manage to notice a lot of them while watching the episodes myself, quite a few of them came from the numerous discussions on the alt.tv.x-files newsgroup. Many more came from the highly informative book *The Truth Is Out There: The Official Guide to the X-Files* by Brian Lowry, as well as articles by Paula Vitaris in *The X-Files* edition of *Cinefantastique* (October 1995). Many more have also been contributed by on-line X-Philes since this list was first published on the newsgroup.

I am quite sure that the list is not yet complete, despite our best efforts, so all additions and/or corrections would be greatly appreciated. Thanks again to everyone who has already added to the list. Please send messages to laura.witte@nashville.com.

WARNING: This list does contain spoilers, but each episode is clearly labeled. Read at your own risk.

This page was last updated on July 28, 1996.

Pilot

1121: Our very first 11:21 — on Scully's clock at the end of the episode. Everyone say it with me now: 11/21 is the birth date of Chris Carter's wife.

1013: I guess the pilot is a good time to mention that the name of Chris Carter's production company, Ten Thirteen productions, is also his very own birth date, 10/13.

1121: Autopsy time: 11:21 (Chris Carter's wife's birthday).

"I made this": The words spoken over the Ten Thirteen company name are spoken by Nathan Couturier, son of the supervising sound editor, Thierry Couturier.

The pilot took place in Bellfleur, Oregon. Chris Carter was born in Bellflower, California.

Ice

The dog in this episode is Blue's father (Blue is David Duchovny's dog and constant companion).

Eve

As Mulder and Scully question mother Ellen Reardon, Eve-girl Cindy Reardon watches a few moments of *Eek the Cat* — a cartoon that later went on to depict Mulder and Scully in cartoon form.

E.B.E.

Tom Braidwood and Val Stefoff — both first assistant directors (and Tom Braidwood is also Frohike) — were names used by Mulder and Scully as aliases to get into the base.

Darkness Falls

Jason Beghe, the actor who plays Ranger Larry Moore, is one of David Duchovny's childhood friends, as well as someone who prodded Duchovny to take up acting (everyone thank him now). ·

Born Again

The actress that portrays Detective Sharon Lazard, Maggie Wheeler, appeared in the movie *New Year's Day* with an un-clothed David Duchovny. The two reportedly dated each other around the time of the movie.

Duane Barry

When Scully stops by the grocery store, she buys pickles and ice cream, an inside reference to her pregnancy.

Ascension

In Mulder's nightmarish vision of Scully (with a rather large stomach) in the clutches of her abductors, that really is Gillian Anderson's stomach. She gave birth to her daughter, Piper, a few weeks after filming this episode.

Mulder's love interest, Kristen Kilar, is played by Perrey Reeves, who was David Duchovny's long-time girlfriend at the time.

Aubrey

Mulder's fascination with women named B.J. might have something to do with Duchovny's then girlfriend,

Perry Reeves, playing a woman named B.J. on *Doogie Howser*.

Paper Clip

10/13: Mulder's birthday is shown as 10/13/60, which mirrors Chris Carter's birth month and day.

Clyde Bruckman's Final Repose

During Mulder's investigation of Clyde Bruckman's psychic gifts, Bruckman holds up a blue piece of cloth and asks if it is from Mulder's New York Knicks t-shirt. This is a reference to the episode "Beyond the Sea," where convicted murderer and psychic Luther Lee Boggs gives a detailed and intricate story after holding a piece of Mulder's New York Knicks t-shirt (that Boggs had thought was the victim's shirt).

The actor who plays "The Stupendous Yappi," Jaap (pronounced Yapp) Broeker, is actually David Duchovny's stand-in, filling in for D.D. when scenes are blocked or lighting is measured.

In the *Space: Above and Beyond* episode titled "R&R" (the one with a guest appearance by David Duchovny himself), Col. McQueen is watching a Clyde Bruckman movie. Perhaps this is writer Glen Morgan's nod to his brother Darin Morgan, the author of Clyde Bruckman's Final Repose?

Nisei

Mulder's second gun reeks of an internet-inside joke, what with all of our discussions on his fumble fingers where guns are concerned.

War of the Coprophages

Breakfast at Tiffany's — the book Scully is reading during one of Mulder's many telephone interruptions

— is also the "Final Jeopardy" answer (or rather question) that was missed by David Duchovny and ended up costing him the game.

Dr. Bambi Berenbaum is named for Dr. May Berenbaum, head of the Entomology Department at the University of Illinois and author of many books on insects.

Syzygy

Grover Cleveland Alexander High School — This was the incorrect answer David Duchovny gave during his infamous appearance on *Jeopardy*.

Jose Chung's From Outer Space (Eth Snafu)

Reynard Muldrake — the pseudonym Jose Chung uses for Mulder. The French word for "fox" is *renard*.

Was the appearance of Alex Trebek yet a third dig at Duchovny for his appearance on *Jeopardy*, or is Mr. Trebek a fan of the show who wanted to appear, or is there something even more sinister afoot?

WetWired

In the home of the woman who shot her neighbor, Scully opens a trunk to find many neatly labeled videotapes — one of which is a tape labeled *Jeopardy*. I wonder if she has the *Celebrity Jeopardy* episode in which David Duchovny appeared?

Yes, Mulder does shoot people

Young at Heart, End Game (the alien doesn't die — but Mulder still shot him), Our Town, Oubliette, Grotesque (not a fatal shot), Pusher (not a fatal shot, but nearly so).

...And Scully shoots people too

Beyond the Sea, Lazarus, Clyde Bruckman's Final Repose.

Address: http:\\www.great-xfiles-info

Yes, Scully does drive

Deep Throat, Ghost in the Machine, Beyond the Sea, E.B.E., Shapes, Irresistable, The Erlenmeyer Flask, Fresh Bones, Clyde Bruckman's Final Repose, 731, War of the Coprophages, Syzygy, Avatar, Quagmire (it's a boat but she still drives it!), Talitha Cumi.

...And Mulder cries

Conduit, The Erlenmeyer Flask (well, his voice breaks), One Breath, End Game, Anasazi, Oubliette, Talitha Cumi.

X-Files & Bathrooms

If you find yourself in an *X-File*, whatever you do, DON'T GO INTO THE BATHROOM! Here are some reasons why (everything listed here occurs in a bathroom).

- Pilot — Scully discovers a couple of mosquito bites
- Deep Throat — Mulder meets Deep Throat
- Squeeze — Scully is attacked by Tooms
- Shadows — Lauren Kyte has an upsetting paranormal vision
- Ghost in the Machine — the CEO gets electrocuted
- Ice — the pilot discovers that he is infected
- Fallen Angel — Max gets apprehended by Mulder & Scully
- Eve — an Eve poisons Mulder & Scully's drinks while they are in the bathroom
- Shapes — Lyle turns into a werewolf
- Roland — Roland has some disturbing visions
- Little Green Men — Mulder finds Jorge
- Host — a man coughs up a fluke while taking a shower
- 3 — Mulder & Kristen kiss
- Red Museum — there's a peeping-Tom behind the bathroom mirror

- Excelsis Dei — Mulder & the nurse are locked in a flooding bathroom
- Aubrey — B.J. discovers the word "sister" carved into her chest
- Irresistable — Pfaster likes for his victims to take baths first
- Die Hand Die Verletzt — Mulder & Scully are to be killed in the shower
- Dod Kalm — toilet water is good for you
- Anasazi — Mulder's father is killed in his bathroom
- 2Shy — Scully is attacked by 2Shy
- 731 — Mulder discovers a murdered scientist
- Revelations — the boy is abducted from the bathroom
- War of the Coprophages — a doctor dies from a burst aneurism while "straining"
- Syzygy — a cheerleader is killed by flying glass
- Piper Maru — Krychek gets the Oil Slick Alien
- Teso Dos Bichos — there are rats in the toilets

Outside In-Jokes

I guess you know that your show has become part of mainstream culture when it starts being referenced by other shows. This is a list of other shows, movies, etc., that mention/reference *The X-Files* (and in doing so make that *X-Files* reference an inside-joke within their own show).

Eek the Cat (Fox, Saturday cartoon show). A cartoon Scully and Mulder finally witness a UFO that even Scully can believe in.

NewsRadio (NBC, Tuesday night comedy). (Someone help me here — I don't remember exactly what happened) The news director called his secretary "Scully" — there was a reason for it, I just don't remember what it was. Reportedly, Dave Foley (the actor who plays the news director) is quite a fan of the show.

Strange Luck (Fox, Friday night drama). The main character's brother knows Mulder, and mentions him in a message left for the main character (Chance Harper).

Independence Day (Fox, blockbuster movie of the summer). A cable company employee admits into the telephone that he likes *The X-Files* too.

Tales from the Crypt: Bordello of Blood (Fox, summer movie). Dennis Miller creates a word: "Duchovnyian."

The Drew Carey Show (ABC, Wednesday night comedy). One of the main characters is a fan of *The X-Files* and mentions the show very frequently (practically in every episode).

Chicago Hope (CBS, Monday night drama). A woman claims to have been impregnated by an alien — *The X-Files'* music plays.

Reboot (ABC, Saturday morning cartoon). "Fax Modem" and "Data Nully" investigate abductions (Gillian Anderson does her own voice). The lighting, camera angles, title sequence, and story line are all very much like a regular *X-Files* episode.

Tag Line Changes

Every so often the line "The Truth Is Out There" during the opening theme is changed. Here are the changes so far:

- The Erlenmeyer Flask — Trust No One
- Ascension — Deny Everything
- Anasazi — EL 'AANIGOO 'AHOOT'E
- 731 — Apology is Policy

X-FILES
EPISODE
SYNOPSES

SEASON ONE

The X-Files: The Pilot

AIR DATE: September 10, 1993
WRITTEN BY: Chris Carter
DIRECTED BY: Robert Mandel

The pilot opens with the words: "The following is inspired by actual documented events," and the series takes off from there. FBI agent Dana Scully is assigned partnership with infamous fellow agent Fox "Spooky" Mulder. Mulder has become so obsessed with paranormal FBI cases known as the X-Files that his superiors are worrying. Agent Scully's job is to watch over, evaluate, and report on her new partner. Mulder, of course, is wary of Scully. The pair travel to Oregon investigating a series of strange murders. An odd metallic device is discovered in the nasal cavity of an exhumed victim. Mulder thinks the murders involve alien abduction; Scully argues for a more rational explanation. The two agents trace the murders to Billy, a near vegetable. They find Billy in the woods where a blinding light suddenly renders him normal again. Scully reports to her superiors that although she believes Mulder's theories, she can't prove them. In the end any record of the case is erased and the Cigarette-Smoking Man is shown depositing the alien device from the nasal cavity into a large bin with other similar devices in an enormous Pentagon warehouse.

Deep Throat

AIR DATE: September 17, 1993

WRITTEN BY: Chris Carter

DIRECTED BY: Daniel Sackheim

Mulder and Scully travel to Ellens Air Force Base in Idaho to investigate the strange disappearences of army test pilots. Mulder is confronted in the bathroom by an FBI higher up, Deep Throat, who claims an interest in the X-Files and warns him off the case. Mulder is sure the government is testing planes built with UFO technology recovered from the famous 1947 Roswell, N.M., crash. After being warned to leave immediately by a group of armed men, and to leave while he still has a job by Scully, Mulder infiltrates a secret area where he finds a UFO. He is captured, strapped to a gurney, and drugged. Scully ignores protocol in order to get Mulder back; she finds him groggy and disoriented. Meeting up with Deep Throat again, Mulder is informed that their lives may be in danger, and that *they* have been here for a very, very long time.

Squeeze

AIR DATE: September 24, 1993

WRITTEN BY: Glen Morgan and James Wong

DIRECTED BY: Harry Longstreet

The X-Files agents are tipped off by an agency buddy of Scully to an unusual case involving three victims whose livers have been removed by hand. There is no clear motive or point of entry. Scully and Mulder can only find an elongated fingerprint near an air vent at the crime scene. They discern that the print matches those found at similar murder scenes, five occurring every thirty years since 1903. It seems the killer will commit two more murders. The agents catch Eugene Tooms attempting to crawl down an air vent at a previous crime scene. After they let him go Mulder realizes his fingerprint — when stretched by computer — matches the elongated one. Tooms slides down a chimney to commit another murder. The agents visit the investigating officer from the past murders. He shows them a thirty-year-old picture of Tooms, who hasn't aged. They then find what appears to be a nest in Tooms' condemned building. Mulder deduces that Tooms is a genetic mutant who emerges from hibernation every thirty years to quell his need for human liver. As Tooms attempts to make Scully his final victim, Mulder bursts in and the agents apprehend the mutant. Tooms is shown in his psychiatric cell building a nest to hibernate in.

Conduit

AIR DATE: October 1, 1993

WRITTEN BY: Alex Gansa and Howard Gordon

DIRECTED BY: Daniel Sackheim

A young girl disappears from a campsite near a UFO hotspot. Mulder is drawn to the case thinking of his own sister's abduction twenty-one years ago. The missing girl is found to be the daughter of a woman who claims to have seen a UFO as a child. Mulder thinks the little brother, Kevin, is the key to finding the girl; he's lately been drawing strange doodles. They find the missing girl's boy-friend in the woods dead. Scully wants to write it off as murder and kidnapping. Later they find the girl herself; she's unconscious and shows signs of prolonged exposure to weightlessness. Her mother steps in and ends the investigation, claiming she doesn't want her daughter to be ridiculed. Mulder cries about his own sister while Scully listens to his old hypnotic regression tapes.

The Jersey Devil

AIR DATE: October 8, 1993

WRITTEN BY: Chris Carter

DIRECTED BY: Joe Napolitano

Mulder and Scully travel to New Jersey to investigate the death of a homeless man found partially eaten by what appear to be human bite marks. Mulder hypothesizes about a man-beast known as the Jersey Devil. Dismissing it as legend, Scully goes to her godson's birthday party. Mulder talks to the homeless and discovers that they have seen the creature and that the police are aware of it. Scully works on her social life while Mulder works on the case. He pursues a beast-woman into the woods. She attacks him but is frightened off by the returning Scully. The beast-woman flees into the woods where she is killed by police. A human bone is found in her digestive system.

Shadows

AIR DATE: October 22, 1993

WRITTEN BY: Glen Morgan and James Wong

DIRECTED BY: Michael Katleman

The X-Files team are called in to examine the bodies of two men, suspected thieves, who were apparently killed by a mysterious force. A video surveillance tape leads them to secretary Lauren Kyte. Her boss, Howard Graves, recently committed suicide. Mulder entertains the possibility of a poltergeist protecting Lauren. Lauren meanwhile is visited by Graves' apparition which cryptically tells her he was murdered. She confronts his old partner, Dorland, and soon after is attacked by two men. They meet the same fate as the suspected thieves. The CIA inform Mulder and Scully that Graves' company is involved in arms dealing with the Middle East and that Graves was murdered by Dorland. Lauren again confronts Dorland in his office. The force attacks him and reveals a hidden computer disk documenting Dorland's crimes.

Ghost in the Machine

AIR DATE: October 29, 1993

WRITTEN BY: Alex Gansa and Howard Gordon

DIRECTED BY: Jerrold Freeman

Mulder's former partner, Jerry Lamana, seeks his help with a case involving an electrocuted CEO who was planning to terminate a high-tech computer operation involving artificial intelligence. Scully and Mulder visit Brad Wilczek, who designed the computer and had a fight with the now dead CEO. Lamana is killed by a plummetting elevator as he goes to arrest Wilczek. Wilczek is shown watching helplessly. Mulder learns from Deep Throat that the Defence Department is interested in Wilczek and his artificial intelligence system. Wilczek informs Mulder how to stop the system and the agents move to implement the computer virus. They encounter trouble from the system itself as well as the Defence Department. Finally, Mulder is able to introduce the virus. The computer's last words are: "Brad, why?"

Ice

AIR DATE: November 5, 1993

WRITTEN BY: Glen Morgan and James Wong

DIRECTED BY: David Nutter

Mulder and Scully, along with scientists Da Silva, Murphy, and Hodge, travel to Icy Cape, Alaska, to investigate the strange behavior of a team of scientists drilling into the arctic core. The final transmission from the remote team shows a crazed team member saying "We are not who we are. It goes no further than this" before he is attacked by another scientist and the two commit suicide together. Arriving at the site, Mulder is attacked by a dog which bites their pilot, Bear. They notice something moving under the dog's skin and dark spots on its skin. Soon Bear discovers the same spots on him. Scully finds a small single-celled organism in all the victims as well as the presence of ammonia in their blood. Bear attacks Mulder and in the scrum Scully notices a worm moving under his skin at the base of his neck. They extract it, killing Bear. Fearing Mulder is also infected, the others lock him up. Scully discovers a cure involving the insertion of a second worm into an infected individual. Believing Mulder is unaffected, she releases him. The others jump him and prepare to "cure" him by inserting the worm in his ear. In the process Hodge notices a worm moving in Da Silva. She runs but is caught and restrained. The worm is inserted and she is cured. After their rescue Mulder wants to return to the site to study the organism but is informed that the military has destroyed the entire facility.

Space

AIR DATE: November 12, 1993

WRITTEN BY: Chris Carter

DIRECTED BY: William Graham

The agents are asked to investigate the possibility of sabotage in the United States' Space Shuttle program. The supervisor of the program, Lt. Col. Belt, an ex-astronaut whose 1977 mission to Mars revealed pictures of a face in that planet's terrain, assures them that all is well. The shuttle launches but soon experiences trouble similar to Belt's '77 mission. A mysterious force causes a car crash as it appears out of the fog and scares the driver. Belt experiences a flashback while alone and an astral body leaves him. In examining records the agents realize that Belt is the saboteur. Belt claims the force possessed and controlled him forcing him to sabotage the program. The shuttle's trajectory is altered to prevent its destruction and Belt, fighting the force, leaps from a window to his death.

Fallen Angel

AIR DATE: November 19, 1993

WRITTEN BY: Alex Gansa and Howard Gordon

DIRECTED BY: Larry Shaw

An alien spacecraft crashes in the woods. The military is on it quickly; they evacuate the area and initiate a cover-up. Deep Thoat tips Mulder off about it, telling him he has

Fallen Angel

twenty-four hours before the scene is "sanitized." Mulder infiltrates the crash site but is captured while photographing the scene. In captivity he meets Max Fenig, a UFO "nut" and fan of Mulder. The military meanwhile search for the UFO pilot. Scully bails Mulder out informing him of the trouble he is in with the FBI higher-ups. Elsewhere, the pilot entity encounters the troops looking for it and burns them severely. Mulder, while holding Fenig through a seizure, notices an incision scar behind his ear similar to scars found on alien abductees. Scully dismisses Max as mentally unstable. Mulder pursues Max into a warehouse where they encounter the alien presence. Max is abducted. On returning to Washington, Mulder is questioned by a hearing committee. After Mulder exits, Deep Throat informs them it would be more dangerous to fire Mulder and have him expose what he knows than to keep him busy with FBI work.

Eve

AIR DATE: December 10, 1993

WRITTEN BY: Kenneth Biller and Chris Brancato

DIRECTED BY: Fred Gerber

Mulder and Scully investigate a pair of bizzare deaths involving two men on opposite coasts of the country who have been drained of their blood. When one victim's eight-year-old daughter, Teena, is kidnapped a few days later, the agents travel to California to protect the other victim's eight-year-old, Cindy. To their amazement they discover the two girls are identical twins. They find that both families were involved in a fertility program with a Dr. Sally Kendrick. They discover the doctor was fired for unauthorised experiments involving genetics. Deep Throat tells Mulder of a top secret genetics experiment which created identical boys called Adam, and girls called Eve. The agents find an identical ringer for Sally Kendrick at a home for the criminally insane; she is called Eve 6. She tells them the Eves were created with extra chromosomes giving them heightened strength and intelligence as well as psychosis. Cindy is kidnapped by a remaining Eve and meets her twin, Teena, for the first time. They admit they already knew of each other and that they are responsible for their fathers' deaths. They poison the Eve who was trying to help them. Now in the care of Mulder and Scully, the girls attempt to poison them as well but are discovered by Mulder in time. The girls are jailed with Eve 6. In the final scene they are visited by Eve 8 who has come for them.

Fire

AIR DATE: December 17, 1993

WRITTEN BY: Chris Carter

DIRECTED BY: Larry Shaw

Phoebe Green, an old flame of Mulder's, asks for his help protecting a visiting British diplomat. Members of Parliament have been getting murdered, each set on fire. Mulder speculates about a pyrokinetic, someone who can control fire. The killer, Cecil L'ively, meanwhile murders and then impersonates the diplomat's caretaker and begins to gain the trust of the family. Scully learns that L'ively had worked for two of the previous victims and is currently in the United States. She confronts L'ively while Mulder rescues the children from fire. L'ively bursts into flames, laughing maniacally. Phoebe douses him with a flame accelerator. Scully narrates that L'ively is recuperating from severe burns and authorities are unsure how to incarcerate him.

AIR DATE: January 7, 1994

WRITTEN BY: Glen Morgan and James Wong

DIRECTED BY: David Nutter

Scully returns to FBI work following the unexpected death of her father from a massive coronary. She and Mulder investigate the kidnappings of two college students and their connection to death row inmate Luther Lee Boggs. Boggs claims he will use his psychic abilities to help find the missing kids in return for a stay of execution. Mulder is skeptical, thinking Boggs is behind the kidnappings and using it to save his life. Scully is intrigued after Boggs relates "psychic" information relating to her father. During an FBI raid Mulder is shot and hospitalized; a suspect who was an old accomplice of Boggs, Lucas Henry, remains missing. Scully returns to Boggs who continues to press for a deal. He tells her he has a message from her father. Scully lies and says she will make the deal. Boggs tells her where to find the boy. She rescues him and Lucas Henry is killed. Scully chooses to forego Boggs' execution, missing her father's message, and she visits Mulder in hospital instead. There she confesses that she is "afraid to believe."

Genderbender

AIR DATE: January 21, 1994

WRITTEN BY: Larry Barber and Paul Barber

DIRECTED BY: Rob Bowman

Mulder and Scully investigate the deaths of three women and two men who suffered massive heart attacks during sex. The agents are led to a strange cult known as the Kindred. One of their members, Andrew, tells Scully about a cult member, Brother Martin, who left "to become one of you." Andrew begins to seduce Scully but Mulder intervenes. The killer picks up another man but police interfere before the murder. The woman transforms into a man, assaults the officer and escapes. The agents track him/her to a motel where, after a struggle, they apprehend him/her. The Kindred help the killer escape. Their house is found deserted and a large crop circle is discovered nearby. Mulder speculates that the cult is actually some kind of extraterrestrial.

Lazarus

AIR DATE: February 4, 1994

WRITTEN BY: Alex Gansa and Howard Gordon

DIRECTED BY: David Nutter

During a bank heist stakeout Scully shoots robber Warren Dupre. At the same time her former lover and fellow agent, Jack Willis, is seriously wounded. When Willis comes to, he has taken on Dupre's consciousness; a tatoo appears on his arm identical to one on Dupre's. Willis informs Scully he knows where Lula, Dupre's wife and accomplice, is hiding out. They go to Lula's but Willis flips out and captures Scully. He proves to Lula that he is Dupre by revealing details about their life together. Willis, a diabetic, collapses in need of insulin. Lula refuses to administer it, admitting she betrayed Dupre out of greed. She ransoms Scully to the FBI for $1 million. The FBI manages to hone in on Scully's location. Willis fakes death, gets Lula's gun, kills her, and then dies; the tatoo disappears.

Young at Heart

AIR DATE: February 11, 1994

WRITTEN BY: Scott Kaufer and Chris Carter

DIRECTED BY: Michael Lange

Mulder's former partner, Reggie Purdue, contacts him in regards to a note found at a recent jewellery store heist. The note is from John Barnett, a crook whose conviction years earlier was due in large part to Mulder's work. Barnett swore revenge on Mulder. According to records, Barnett died in prison four years ago; the handwriting however is a perfect match. Mulder's investigation uncovers experiments performed by a Dr. Ridley, who pronounced Barnett dead; Ridley also had his medical licence revoked for research malpractice. Ridley had experimented on Barnett, replacing his hand by growing a new one from salamander cells. Ridley tells Scully that his work was financed by the government. Mulder learns via Deep Throat that the government is interested in Ridley's work and is trying to obtain vital research from Barnett. Barnett meanwhile vows to continue killing Mulder's friends. His fingerprints are discovered on Scully's answering machine. He follows Scully to a cello recital where agents stake him out. Barnett shoots at Scully but she is protected by a bulletproof vest. He escapes into the hallway where he is shot and killed by Mulder. Mulder fears they "haven't seen the last of John Barnett."

E.B.E.

AIR DATE: February 18, 1994

WRITTEN BY: Glen Morgan and James Wong

DIRECTED BY: William Graham

A UFO is shot down by an Iraqi pilot near a U.S. base. A truck driver is soon witness to a UFO; Mulder believes he was transporting an E.B.E. (extraterrestrial biological entity). Looking for more information, Mulder takes Scully to see a group of conspiracy watchdogs known as the Lone Gunmen. Deep Throat gives Mulder a false tip and when confronted about it states that there "still exist some secrets that should remain secret." Mulder and Scully locate the truck in Washington State where they see a blinding light similar to alien encounters. It turns out to be another hoax designed as a diversion. Following the truck driver they infiltrate a government facility but are soon halted by security. Deep Throat is there and tells Mulder of a secret pact made between countries that any E.B.E. be exterminated. Deep Throat himself exterminated E.B.E.'s when he was with the CIA. He tells Mulder that he is using him to atone for the guilt he feels from those incidents. Mulder wonders aloud which lies to believe.

Miracle Man

AIR DATE: March 18, 1994

WRITTEN BY: Howard Gordon and Chris Carter

DIRECTED BY: Michael Lange

When people touched by Samuel, a miracle faith healer, start dying, Mulder and Scully are called in to probe the Miracle Ministry. They find Samuel in a bar, believing his gift corrupted. He also knows things about Mulder's abducted sister, causing Mulder to see recurring visions of her throughout the episode. During Samuel's hearing the courtroom fills with locusts. Once free Samuel tries to heal a woman in a wheelchair. She goes into convulsions and dies. The autopsy reveals poison. The agents discover that the locust plague was in fact the work of a human. In the meantime Samuel is beaten to death in jail. The agents trace the locusts to a man Samuel had saved from severe burns, Leonard Vance. He is angry he was saved and now remains horribly disfigured. He commits suicide when Samuel

appears to him in a vision. Samuel's body goes missing; a
nurse claims she saw him walk out.

Shapes

AIR DATE: April 1, 1994

WRITTEN BY: Marilyn Osborne

DIRECTED BY: David Nutter

A young man, Lyle Parker, is attacked and wounded by a
creature before it is shot and killed by his father. The
creature turns out to be Joe Goodensnake, a Native American whose reservation is involved in boundary disputes
with the Parkers. Mulder hypothesizes about werewolves
and explains to Scully that the very first X-File stemmed
from similar events in the area. A look at Joe Goodensnake's teeth reveals wolf-like fangs. Lyle's father is
attacked by a creature on his porch. Lyle is found naked
and unconscious nearby. Scully takes him to the hospital
and then for questioning. In the meantime Mulder consults
a tribal elder who tells him of a wolf-like creature known
as the Manitou. Calling the hospital, Mulder learns that
Scully and Lyle have left for the ranch, and that traces of
the father's blood were found in Lyle — traces that could
only get there through ingestion. Lyle meanwhile morphs
into the creature and attacks Scully. Mulder arrives with
the Sheriff just in time to shoot the creature, which again
becomes Lyle Parker.

Darkness Falls

AIR DATE: April 15, 1994

WRITTEN BY: Chris Carter

DIRECTED BY: Joe Napolitano

After thirty loggers vanish in a scenario similar to one from sixty years previous, Mulder and Scully venture to Washington State's forest to investigate. The logging company suspects eco-terrorists are responsible. The agents find a huge cocoon in the woods. Inside is a man whose blood has been drained. Doug Spinney, an eco-terrorist, tells them of a nocturnal force that eats people alive. By cutting down old growth trees the loggers inadvertently freed centuries-old green mites. The logging company security officer leaves the agents and is caught and devoured by the mites. Spinney goes for help, leaving Mulder, Scully, and the Ranger alone for the night. Their generator fails but just in time the sun rises. Spinney returns but flees as mites swarm him. Later Mulder, Scully, and the Ranger are discovered in a cocoon. They are treated and told that the bugs will be eradicated by a series of burns and pesticides. Mulder asks what if that doesn't work and is told that is not an option.

Tooms

AIR DATE: April 22, 1994

WRITTEN BY: Glen Morgan and James Wong

DIRECTED BY: David Nutter

Eugene Victor Tooms, the liver-eating mutant from *Squeeze*, is up for parole based on the results of a psychiatric hearing and a slow-witted, sympathetic psychiatrist. Despite Mulder's frantic warnings, the panel releases Tooms. Meanwhile Scully meets with Skinner and the Cigarette-Smoking Man. She is warned against "unorthodox investigative procedures." On a tip from Frank Briggs, the detective who investigated the previous Tooms murders, Scully finds the body of a Tooms victim from sixty years ago. Mulder foils a murder attempt while tailing

Tooms but the mutant wriggles away. Allowing Scully to continue the surveillance, Mulder goes home to rest, with Tooms hiding in his trunk. Tooms sneaks in to Mulder's apartment and makes it look like Mulder assaulted him. Skinner forbids Mulder from going near Tooms and advises a vacation. An examination of the sixty-year-old skeleton reveals Tooms' teeth marks. Meanwhile Tooms' psychiatrist visits him and the psychiatrist has his liver eaten. The agents find the body and deduce Tooms will return to his old abode. The site is now a shopping mall. Mulder crawls under an escalator where he finds Tooms' nest. The mutant attacks him and, after a struggle, Mulder turns the escalator on, crushing Tooms. While reading the report Skinner asks the Cigarette-Smoking Man if he believes it. He replies, "Of course I do."

Born Again

AIR DATE: April 29, 1994

WRITTEN BY: Alex Gansa and Howard Gordon

DIRECTED BY: Jerrold Freedman

Mulder and Scully are called in after a detective, Barbala, plummets to his death from a room where he was watching a lost little girl. The little girl, Michelle, claims another man was in the room. The description she gives matches Charlie Morris, a murdered detective. Mulder poses a theory that Michelle is the reincarnation of Charlie Morris. They find she has mutilated her dolls to match what was done to Morris' body. Later she is present at the strange death of another former detective. The two dead cops and Morris' old partner, Fiore, were all involved in murdering Morris. Michelle confronts Fiore and is about to kill him when Mulder and Scully burst in and stop her.

Fiore admits his part in Morris' death; the two other deaths are ruled as accidental, and Michelle returns to normal. Her mother refuses Mulder's pleas to study her further. The case is closed, unsolved.

Roland

AIR DATE: May 6, 1994

WRITTEN BY: Chris Ruppenthal

DIRECTED BY: David Nutter

The X-Files team investigates the deaths of two research scientists working on a jet engine. Only a retarded janitor named Roland was on hand when the second man was fatally sucked into the engine. Mulder notices and takes a piece of paper on which Roland has been scribbling a number series. Soon Roland murders another one of the scientists, Dr. Keats. It is discovered that someone has been working on the project using the computer password of Dr. Grable, the first dead scientist. The password matches Roland's number series. The agents find that Roland and Grable are twins and that Grable's head has been preserved through cryogenics. Mulder considers the idea that the twins may have shared a psychic bond and that perhaps Grable is manipulating Roland to murder the other scientists. Roland runs when Mulder and Scully try to question him. The only survivor of the original team, Nollette, begins to thaw Grable's head while Roland, in the lab, reaches a breakthrough in the research. Nolette enters and is attacked by Roland who locks him in the engine chamber. Mulder and Scully arrive in time to coax Roland into shutting down the engine before it sucks in and kills Nollette.

The Erlenmeyer Flask

AIR DATE: May 13, 1994

WRITTEN BY: Chris Carter

DIRECTED BY: R.W. Goodwin

Deep Throat tips Mulder off to a case involving a fugitive man with superhuman strength who bleeds green liquid. Mulder traces the fugitive's car to a Dr. Berube who refuses to talk. The agents wonder if Deep Throat's tip is for real; he tells them they've "never been closer." A crew-cut man kills Dr. Berube; Scully takes his work to a scientist, Dr. Carpenter, who finds that Berube was cloning bacteria similar to plant cells. The DNA however contains extraterrestrial elements. Mulder, in the meantime, is contacted by the fugitive and led to a warehouse where he finds five men in strange, fluid-filled containers. Armed men chase him away. Scully tells Mulder that for the first time she doesn't know what to believe. Upon returning to the warehouse they find it empty. Deep Throat explains that what Mulder saw was an experiment testing alien viruses on terminal patients. It has likely been destroyed by covert groups instructed by the FBI leaders. They are told they must find Dr. Secare, one of the experimenters, before the others do. Mulder, working alone, finds Secare, but the Crew-Cut Man takes him hostage and kills Secare. Deep Throat plans an exchange of alien tissue for Mulder. Insisting on making the exchange, Deep Throat is shot. His last words are: "Trust no one." Mulder calls Scully two weeks later to say the X-Files have been shut down. He adds that his work will continue as long as "the truth is out there." As in the pilot, the episode ends with the Cigarette-Smoking Man depositing an alien fetus in an enormous Pentagon warehouse.

SEASON TWO

Little Green Men

AIR DATE: September 16, 1994

WRITTEN BY: Glen Morgan and James Wong

DIRECTED BY: David Nutter

The investigation of the X-Files has been officially ceased; Mulder and Scully have been reassigned. Mulder meets with a "friend" in Washington, Senator Matheson, who enlightens him as to a recent alien visitaion in Puerto Rico. The Senator tells him he must make contact within twenty-four hours, before a UFO retrieval team is dispatched. The Cigarette-Smoking Man and Skinner track Mulder by way of Scully, knowing she will find him. She heads to San Juan, losing the agents tailing her. Mulder meanwhile meets a frightened Spanish man who draws an alien face. Upon hearing a shrill noise the man flees into the jungle where he is found dead. Later, in the Spanish man's room, Mulder encounters a bright light and an alien figure blows open a bolted door. Scully arrives to find Mulder unconscious. He tells her of the tapes and printouts he has made of the recent encounter. Just then troops arrive and the agents must run. Mulder is raked over the coals by Skinner; The Cigarette-Smoking Man tells him, "Your time is over." Mulder finds his tape is blank and realizes he still lacks proof of his alien encounter. He tells Scully that, although he no longer has the X-Files, he still has his work, her, and himself.

Little Green Men

The Host

AIR DATE: September 23, 1994

WRITTEN BY: Chris Carter

DIRECTED BY: Daniel Sackheim

Mulder is assigned the case of a man found dead in the sewer. Thinking he's being punished, he complains to Skinner and tells Scully he's thinking about leaving the FBI. He receives an anonymous call telling him he "has a friend at the FBI," and that success in this case is necessary for reinstatement of the X-Files. Scully finds a large parasitic worm, known as a fluke, while performing an autopsy on the sewer corpse. Meanwhile a sewer worker is pulled under water and attacked. He emerges alive but with an odd wound on his back. Later, in the shower, he convulses and purges another fluke worm that swims down the drain. While Mulder is looking around a sewage treatment plant, something large is seen swimming in the water. The system is flushed and they discover a being which is half man–half fluke. Reporting to Skinner, Mulder is surprised to be told the case should have been an X-File. Another anonymous tip informs Scully that the first victim is Russian. The flukeman, meanwhile, kills a driver transporting him to an institution, and escapes into a sewage tanker. Mulder chases the tanker to a treatment plant where he determines the creature is trying to swim out to sea. After a struggle in the sewage, Mulder releases a gate on the fleeing flukeman, cutting him in half. Scully realizes the flukeman was likely caused by radioactive waste from Chernobyl. The remains of the flukeman meanwhile rise to the ocean surface where its eyes open.

Blood

AIR DATE: September 30, 1994

WRITTEN BY: Glen Morgan and James Wong

DIRECTED BY: David Nutter

A real estate salesman goes on a killing rampage before dying himself, after he reads the words "KILL 'EM ALL" on an elevator's digital display. Mulder is called to investigate. This is the seventh killing spree in an otherwise peacefull small town. A destroyed electronic device has been found at each crime scene. Meanwhile a local woman goes berserk after seeing a similar readout and kills a mechanic. Mulder and Sheriff Spencer go to her house but Spencer shoots her as she attacks Mulder. Autopsy reveals severely abnormal levels of adrenaline plus an unknown substance. The Lone Gunmen inform Mulder about LSDM, an experimental insecticide which causes the fear instinct in insects. Mulder discovers the town is using the chemical and figures that something, or someone, is sending digital messages which increase existing phobias, resulting in murder. They are led to a laid-off postal worker, Ed Funsch, who snaps and begins firing randomly from a tower. When apprehended he tells Mulder "they" wouldn't let him sleep. Later Mulder finds the message "ALL DONE. BYE BYE." on his cellular phone readout; it appears the experiment is finished.

Sleepless

AIR DATE: October 7, 1994

WRITTEN BY: Howard Gordon

DIRECTED BY: Rob Bowman

Mulder finds a tape hidden in his morning paper tipping him off to a case where a scientist was seemingly burnt to death but with no signs of fire. He is assigned a new partner, Alex Krycek. They discover that the scientist, Dr. Grissom, ran a sleep disorder clinic. Meanwhile a man is shot to death by an image of Vietnamese peasants. The man was a Marine who had been stationed in the same area that Grissom worked at in Vietnam. The only survivor from that unit has recently gone missing from a V.A. hospital. His name is Augustus Cole; he hasn't slept in twenty-four years. X tells Mulder of a secret project designed to do away with the need for sleep in soldiers; the resulting unit began to murder randomly. Cole is now seeking revenge for those experiments. Mulder theorizes that Cole has developed an ability to kill through psychic powers affecting dreams. Mulder goes to protect the other doctor who was involved but Cole "shoots" him with his powers. Later Mulder catches him and begs him to testify against what the army did. Krycek however shoots and kills Cole, claiming he saw a gun. Krycek later meets with the Cigarette-Smoking Man, telling him that Mulder has another source in place of Deep Throat and that Scully is a larger problem than was described. The Cigarette-Smoking Man replies, "Every problem has a solution."

Duane Barry
(Part 1 of 2)

AIR DATE: October 14, 1994

WRITTEN BY: Chris Carter

DIRECTED BY: Chris Carter

Opening in 1985, we see Duane Barry being abducted by aliens and screaming "not again!" Back to 1994, and Barry, in a treatment facility, is insisting they're coming back for him. He takes four people hostage, wanting witnesses to go to the abduction site. While Mulder negotiates, Barry

shoots a hostage; he agrees to let the wounded man go in
exchange for Mulder. Scully determines that Barry is an
ex-FBI agent who, since being shot in the head, is violent
and delusional. Barry tells Mulder about government
abduction cover-ups and describes the abduction site in
detail. An FBI marksman wounds Barry. Examination
seems to back up the abduction story as pieces of metal
are discovered in Barry's body. On impulse Scully scans a
piece of this metal at the supermarket. The register goes
nuts; Barry jolts awake in hopital and escapes. As Scully is
leaving a message on Mulder's answering machine, Barry
crashes through her window and she screams into the
phone for help. *To be continued . . .*

Ascension
(Part 2 of 2)

AIR DATE: October 21, 1994

WRITTEN BY: Paul Brown

DIRECTED BY: Michael Lange

Mulder hears Scully's message and is visited by a frantic
Mrs. Scully who dreamt Dana was taken away. Duane
Barry, with Scully in his trunk, drives off and kills a patrol-
man who pulls him over. Mulder takes off for Skyland
Mountain, where he deduces Barry is headed. Krycek
informs the Cigarette-Smoking Man where they are going.
Mulder is stranded in a mountain tram by Krycek who kills
the operator. He manages to escape the tram and finds
Barry's car, empty but for Scully's golden cross. Barry,
alone, runs up yelling that he's free. He tells Mulder that
"they" took Scully, that he traded her to "them" but didn't
harm her. Mulder attacks him and is told the military is in
on it. As they return to see Krycek, Barry dies in convulsions. Krycek is told by the Cigarette-Smoking Man that

he must keep Mulder's trust and they can't kill him. Taking Krycek's car, Mulder notices ashes in the ash tray and links them to the Cigarette-Smoking Man. Krycek suddenly disappears. Skinner reluctantly reopens the X-Files.

3

AIR DATE: November 4, 1994

WRITTEN BY: Chris Ruppenthal, Glen Morgan, and James Wong

DIRECTED BY: David Nutter

With Scully still missing, Mulder shows up at a recent crime scene similar to a number of cases across the country he has been following. He figures it is the work of a cult who drain their victim's blood. He apprehends a suspect at a blood bank whom he catches drinking blood. When the suspect asks him if he doesn't want to live forever, Mulder quips: "Not if draw-string pants come back in style." Thinking the suspect is delusional about his vampire beliefs, and hoping fear will make him talk, Mulder locks him in a room where the rising sun will eventually engulf the room. They find the suspect, John, burnt to death by the sunlight. A stamp on John's hand leads Mulder to a Hollywood night-club where he meets Kristen (played by Duchovny's then girlfriend Perrey Reeves). She leaves with another man when Mulder refuses to taste her blood. When Mulder follows, the guy beats him up. The man is soon found dead, and with three sets of human bite marks on him. Finding Kristen again Mulder realizes she is not part of the cult anymore but that the others are after her. They spend the night together and in the morning John has returned. Mulder manages to escape with Kristen and they kill the female cult leader. Since they can be killed only by their own kind, Kristen tastes her own blood, becomes one, and torches the house. Four bodies are found, and Mulder is again alone.

One Breath

AIR DATE: November 11, 1994

WRITTEN BY: Glen Morgan and James Wong

DIRECTED BY: R.W. Goodwin

In speaking with Scully's mother, Mulder announces emphatically that they musn't give up looking for Dana. Scully turns up mysteriously at a Washington Hospital. She is shown floating on a lake in a small boat, tethered to a dock as if in a parallel world. The Lone Gunmen discover that Scully's DNA has been experimented on. Later, a man steals Scully's blood sample, and Mulder runs after him. X interrupts the chase and winds up executing the man. Meanwhile Skinner is told to sit on Mulder by the Cigarette-Smoking Man. When he leaves, Mulder confronts Skinner telling him the Cigarette-Smoking Man is behind Scully's disappearance. Mulder locates the Cigarette-Smoking Man and confronts him but learns nothing. Feeling guilty over what happened to Scully, Mulder hands in his resignation to Skinner who refuses it. X tells Mulder that some men will be ransacking his apartment tonight and he can kill them in revenge for Scully's abduction. Scully's sister Melissa however convinces Mulder to go to the hospital as Scully's condition is weakening. He returns to find his apartment ransacked and the men already gone. Scully awakens and seems okay. The two agents have an emotional scene. Later, when Scully asks for a Nurse Owens who tended to her in intensive care, she is told that there is no Nurse Owens working at the hospital.

Firewalker

AIR DATE: November 18, 1994

WRITTEN BY: Howard Gordon

DIRECTED BY: David Nutter

Scully returns to action when a group of research scientists exploring a volcano's core send a distress signal and a video tape shows a scientist dead. At the site Mulder is attacked by one of the survivors. The group — Ludwig, Tanaka, and O'Neil — fear the team leader, Trepkos, has gone mad and will kill them. While going over Trepkos' notes Mulder finds mention of a new life-form which can live in the incredible temperatures of the earth's core. Trepkos meanwhile attacks and kills a scientist saying, "No one can leave." When Tanaka collapses they attempt to transfer him to hospital, but he runs off. From the crest of a ravine the others watch as a form bursts from his throat. Scully identifies it as a spore which grew to maturity in his body. Mulder and Ludwig search for Trepkos who attacks and kills Ludwig. He burns the body in an attempt to kill the spore which infected the others when a robot returned with it from the Earth's core. Scully determines the spore must be inhaled. O'Neil is suddenly overtaken by the spore and handcuffs herself to Scully. Scully manages to evade the bursting spore by shutting O'Neil in a chamber. The agents leave Trepkos there, saying there were no survivors.

Red Museum

AIR DATE: December 9, 1994

WRITTEN BY: Chris Carter

DIRECTED BY: Win Phelps

The X-Files team are called to investigate when missing teens begin to reappear hysterical with fear, in their underwear, and with the words "HE IS ONE" scrawled on their backs. The Sheriff suspects a local vegetarian cult known as the Church of the Red Museum. Tests show the presence of an opiate in the blood of a recent female victim. Odin, the leader of the Red Museum, is arrested along with a former doctor. Mulder and Scully are led by an old town resident to a farm where they see growth hormones used on cattle. The old man believes there is a link between the hormone and a string of recent violence. When it is discovered that a Dr. Larsen has treated the abductees with vitamin shots since childhood, and a briefcase full of money turns up with his corpse, Scully links him to the conspiracy. Deep Throat's murderer, the Crew-Cut Man, returns and kills a man injecting cattle wih the hormone. The Sheriff's son is found dead. Mulder realizes that a local landlord, Gerd Thomas, has been abducting the kids. Thomas claims Dr. Larsen's tests made monsters of the teens. The substance is found to be alien DNA, the same stuff featured in *The Erlenmeyer Flask* episode. Realizing the town has been part of an experiment which is now being covered up, Mulder takes the kids to Red Museum for safety. There he encounters the Crew-Cut Man who is shot and killed by the Sheriff; he has no official identity. The case remains unsolved.

Excelsius Dei

AIR DATE: December 16, 1994

WRITTEN BY: Paul Brown

DIRECTED BY: Stephen Surjik

Mulder and Scully are called in to investigate after a nurse in a convalescent home is raped by an unseen force. She blames seventy-four-year-old patient Hal Arden who laughs it off. Later that night Hal's roommate, Stan, tells him to be careful or he'll ruin things. Soon after Hal is choked to death by an invisible hand. In the hotel, Mulder is shown watching porno movies, which he tells Scully are "definitely not his." The agents return to the home in time to see an orderly be thrown out a window by an unseen force, but Stan is present. Mulder discovers that an Asian orderly named Gung has been treating the patients with mushrooms, and he also finds the body of a missing orderly. Gung claims that the people who died at the home are now haunting it. He realizes his mushroom stash has gone missing. While Mulder theorizes about the possibility that some spirit has been unleashed, he is locked in a flooding bathroom. Stan goes into seizure and Mulder breaks free. Gung is deported and the patients return to their vegetative state.

Aubrey

AIR DATE: January 6, 1995

WRITTEN BY: Sara Charno

DIRECTED BY: Rob Bowman

Policewoman B.J. Morrow, in the midst of an affair and pregnancy, finds herself inexplicably digging up the skeleton of an FBI agent missing since 1942. Mulder and Scully travel to Aubrey, Missouri, to investigate this find. The dead agent had been investigating a serial killer who carved the word "SISTER" into the chest of his victims; the case was never solved. The crimes have begun to occur again. B.J. finds an old mug shot of Harry Cokely; it turns out he was convicted of rape in 1945 and had carved the word "SISTER" on his victim. She identifies Cokely as the man in the visions she has been having. Cokely, however, is an old man and seems incapable of committing the recent crimes. B.J. awakens from a nightmare to find "SISTER" carved on her chest. She rushes to a house where she finds another missing FBI agent in the floorboards; Cokely lived in the house fifty years ago. Mulder and Scully find out Cokely's rape victim had become pregnant and gave the baby up for adoption. Mulder hypothesizes about the collective unconscious; perhaps the genetic memory of Cokely's descendent is causing him to murder. The agents find out that B.J. is the granddaughter of Cokely. They rush to protect the rape victim, but find that although B.J. was there, she has gone after Cokely. She attacks Mulder at Cokely's house. As Cokely dies, B.J. snaps out of her "trance" and drops her blade. The episode ends with B.J. under suicide watch in an institution after attempting to abort her unborn child.

Irresistable

AIR DATE: January 13, 1995

WRITTEN BY: Chris Carter

DIRECTED BY: David Nutter

Mulder takes a case involving a desecrated grave in Minneapolis becuse he has tickets to the Redskins-Vikings football game. He doesn't think the case is an X-File, only a fetishist who might turn to murder in order to satisfy his corpse fetish. Meanwhile, Donnie, a mortuary worker, kills a prostitute and takes pieces of her body. When he tries to get another girl, she escapes resulting in Donnie's arrest. Scully has a nightmare relating to the case. Donnie is released after a cellmate gives him Scully's name. She returns to Washington and admits to her counsellor how much the case is bothering her. Police meanwhile search Donnie's apartment and find body parts. Back in Minneapolis, Donnie ambushes Scully and holds her captive.

Mulder tracks them down. Scully breaks free during a ritual bath. While they wrestle, Mulder breaks in with reinforcements. Scully breaks down and cries on Mulder's shoulder.

Die Hand Die Verletzt

AIR DATE: January 27, 1995

WRITTEN BY: Glen Morgan and James Wong

DIRECTED BY: Kim Manners

A Parent-Teacher Committee meeting ends with candles and a prayer to Satan. Later, two couples enter the woods and read a similar prayer. A boy is found dead, his heart and eyes removed. Mulder and Scully are told by the local Sheriff of old stories involving Satan worshippers in the town. Scully dismisses the idea that the place is "weird" but isn't so sure when toads fall from the sky and water drains backwards. The PTC meets again and Calcagni, a member, says he believes a "presence" is responsible for the murder. A new substitute teacher, Mrs. Paddock, is shown to have the boy's heart and eyes in her desk. While her class dissects pigs, one girl, Shannon, freaks out. She reveals to Mulder and Scully horrific stories of Satanic ritual involving her and her little sister. She blames her stepfather, Jim Ausbury, a member of the PTC. Returning to Mrs. Paddock's lab to continue the dissection, Shannon is controlled by Mrs. Paddock into slashing her own wrists. Ausbury admits to Satanic rituals but says that they skipped over the more disturbing parts. Paddock sends Mulder a fake call saying Scully is in trouble. He handcuffs Ausbury to a basement railing and leaves. Soon a giant python enters and devours Ausbury whole. The agents return to find only bones. The PTC plan to sacrifice the agents to save themselves. They jump the agents and prepare to kill them but Calcagni, under the control of Paddock, turns the gun on the others, then himself. Mulder and Scully find the message "Goodbye. It's been nice working with you." written on the chalkboard. There is no sign of Paddock.

Fresh Bones

AIR DATE: February 3, 1995

WRITTEN BY: Howard Gordon

DIRECTED BY: Rob Bowman

Mulder and Scully investigate the deaths of two soldiers at a Haitian refugee camp. There is talk of a voodoo curse involved. Colonel Wharton tells them the soldiers are hated by the refugees and so are under heavy stress. Scully discovers the latest victim's corpse, a Private McAlpin, has been replaced by the body of a dog. The agents find a figure walking in the road — it's McAlpin. A soldier tells Mulder and Scully that a refugee named Bauvais warned Wharton he would take his men if they weren't allowed to go home. Bauvais is beaten to death by Wharton. X tells Mulder that Wharton is seeking revenge from his mission in Haiti. The soldier who helped the agents turns up dead in Mulder's room; McAlpin is there with a bloody knife. The agents find out both of the dead soldiers filed complaints about Wharton before their deaths. Mulder witnesses Wharton performing a voodoo ritual over Bauvais' coffin. Bauvais rises and blows powder at Wharton, killing him. While the agents leave, Wharton is shown in his coffin alive and screaming.

Colony
(Part 1 of 2)

AIR DATE: February 10, 1995

WRITTEN BY: Chris Carter

STORY BY: David Duchovny
and Chris Carter

DIRECTED BY: Nick Marck

The episode begins with Mulder being rushed into Emergency suffering from severe hypothermia. Scully warns the doctors that the cold is what is keeping him alive. Flashback two weeks ago, to a government research vessel. It discovers a strange ship crashing in the Arctic Circle. The rescued pilot kills an abortion clinic doctor who bleeds a green, frothy liquid. Mulder receives three separate obituaries, all of identical abortion doctors with no records of birth. He finds another of the identical men and sends a field agent to protect him. The field agent encounters the pilot and shoots him; the pilot bleeds the same green blood. It causes the agent's blood to coagulate instantly, killing him. As the X-Files team arrives, the pilot morphs into the field agent and escapes. A CIA agent, Ambrose Chapel, approaches Mulder. He claims the doctors are part of a Soviet cloning experiment. The next doctor they encounter, terrified of Chapel, jumps out a window and runs away. Chapel, who is the pilot transformed, catches and kills the man, leaving a pool of green fluid. Mulder is summoned to his parents' house where he finds Samantha, his missing sister. She tells him the clones are her adopted, alien parents and that they are being hunted by an alien bounty hunter who can resemble anything. Only Samantha can identify him. Scully meanwhile finds the remaining doctors and places them in protective custody. The pilot, in disguise, kills them all. Mulder shows up at her hotel room door; while he's in her room she gets a phone call, from Mulder. *To be continued . . .*

End Game

AIR DATE: February 17, 1995

WRITTEN BY: Frank Spotnitz

DIRECTED BY: Rob Bowman

Scully realizes the man in her room is not Mulder and pulls her gun on him. He overpowers her and takes her hostage wanting to trade for Samantha. Samantha tells Mulder the clones stem from two alien visitors trying to start an earth colony. The bounty hunter was sent because their experiment is unauthorized. A trade is organized where a sharpshooter will target the pilot. The plan goes awry and Samantha and the pilot plummet off a bridge into icy water. Mulder is devastated but follows instructions given by Samantha if any thing happened to her. He finds a group of Samantha clones. They admit they used him but also tell him they know where his sister really is. The bounty hunter breaks in and knocks Mulder out. He awakens to an empty, burning building. X tells him the pilot has gone back to his craft in the arctic, and Mulder follows. Scully asks Skinner for help; she also contacts X but is refused any information. Skinner and X battle and soon Skinner is at Scully's door with the information. Mulder fights with the bounty hunter who leaves him to die on the Arctic ice. Shift back to the beginning of *Colony*; Mulder is rushed into emergency with hypothermia. Scully saves his life keeping him cold so the alien virus can't take effect. Recovering in bed he tells Scully, "I found something I thought maybe I'd lost: faith to keep looking."

Fearful Symmetry

AIR DATE: February 24, 1995

WRITTEN BY: Stevan DeJarnatt

DIRECTED BY: James Whitmore Jr.

Mulder wonders if an escaped zoo elephant could be responsible for damage done downtown by an invisible force. He and Scully meet with Ed Meecham, head zoo-keeper; his new superior, Willa Ambrose; and the head of an animal rights group, Kyle Lang. The Lone Gunmen inform Mulder that the area is a UFO hotspot and that the zoo has never had a successful pregnancy. Scully believes the animal rights group is somehow behind things, and she tails a member who breaks into the zoo. In a flash of light a tiger is free of its cage and mauls the man to death. Questioning Sophie, a gorilla who knows sign language, they find she is afraid of a light. An autopsy on the elephant reveals it was pregnant, though it was never mated; the same is true of the tiger. Mulder wonders about alien abduction and artificial insemination. The zoo is closed and Sophie is to be transferred. Mulder, tracking Meecham, winds up locked in Sophie's cage. She is panicked and attacks him. In a bright light Mulder sees her disappear. Her final signs are "Man Save Man." Sophie turns up miles away; she dies. Mulder is left wondering if the abductions are meant as a means of conservation to combat extinction.

Dod Kalm

AIR DATE: March 10, 1995

WRITTEN BY: Alex Gansa and Howard Gordon

DIRECTED BY: Rob Bowman

Survivors of an abandoned U.S. Navy Destroyer are found in the Norwegian Sea 42 hours after they jumped ship.

Scully sneaks into a military hospital to see a survivor and notices he looks ninety years old even though he's only twenty-eight. Mulder wonders about a wrinkle in time and the infamous Philadelphia Experiment. Other ships have also disappeared in that area. The agents board the Destroyer in Norway. It is corroded as if it is a *very* old ship. Once on board they find mumified corpses, but their boat is stolen, leaving them stranded aboard the Destroyer. They locate the captain who has become a drunk, and he soon dies of old age, even though he is only thirty-five. The captain who brought them, Trondheim, is attacked by a pirate whaler named Olaffson. The agents and Trondhiem awake to find themselves aged thirty years. They realize their plight stems from contaminated water. Mulder is worst off due to his seasickness. The only clean water on board is in the sewage system. Trondhiem selfishly locks himself in the sewage hold to horde the water. He is drowned as the ship begins to flood. Mulder loses consciousness while Scully writes in a journal. They awaken in hospital, rescued by Navy Seals and saved by the information in Scully's log.

Humbug

AIR DATE: March 31, 1995

WRITTEN BY: Darin Morgan

DIRECTED BY: Kim Manners

When Jerald Glazebrook, an alligator man in a circus sideshow, is killed in his pool by a mysterious creature, Mulder and Scully travel to Florida to investigate. The attack is similar to forty-eight others spanning twenty-eight years with no known motives or suspects. The agents check into a trailer park in a town comprised of sideshow performers. The park is run by Mr. Nutt, a midget, and

Lanny, whose twin brother, Leonard, grows out of his side. Soon the creature kills another victim. Mulder sees a strange man, covered in tattoo puzzle pieces eating a live fish in the river. It turns out to be the Conundrum, a circus geek who eats anything. Later Mr. Nutt is attacked and killed. The agents bring a suspect, Dr. Blockhead, in for questioning. At the jail they discover Lanny's twin brother, Leonard, has disjoined himself and is "looking for another brother," but is inadvertently killing people. Mulder and Scully chase the twin creature but he escapes. Leonard attempts to attack the Conundrum; when the agents arrive, the Conundrum, unhurt, is seen rubbing his stomach, digesting. Lanny dies of liver cirrhosis and Leonard is never found. As Blockhead and the Conundrum drive off, Mulder asks what's wrong with the sickly-looking Conundrum. He replies, "Probably something I ate."

The Calusari

AIR DATE: April 14, 1995

WRITTEN BY: Sara Charno

DIRECTED BY: Michael Vejar

Mulder investigates a three-month-old murder in which a small child was lured onto traintracks by a balloon pulled by what appears to be a poltergeist. Speaking with the boy's parents, Scully notices the Romanian grandmother drawing a swastika on their other son Charlie's hand. The old woman yells at the mother, "You marry a devil! You have devil child!" The father, Steve, agrees to take the boy to a social worker which upsets the mother and grandmother. The garage door opener catches his tie as he attempts to leave with Charlie and he is hanged. Two dead roosters are discovered in the old woman's room along with other strange things. She gives Charlie to three men

in suits who ritualistically conjure up an image of Charlie
who curses them in Romanian. The grandmother locks
herself in a room with Charlie. Objects begin to fly and
she is knocked down. The two roosters are brought back
to life by Charlie and peck the old woman to death. Under
questioning the three men in suits, who are known as the
Calusari, say they are trying to exorcise the house of evil.
Charlie cries to a social worker that "Michael" killed his
grandmother. It turns out Michael was Charlie's stillborn
twin brother. Charlie is hospitalized but Michael attacks a
nurse and asks to be taken home. Scully pursues Michael
while Mulder gets help from the Calusari who perform a
ritual at the hospital. Just as Michael is about to kill Scully,
the Calusari ritual finishes and Michael vanishes. In Mulder's voiceover he states the case remains unsolved.

F. Emasculata

AIR DATE: April 28, 1995

WRITTEN BY: Chris Carter and Howard Gordon

DIRECTED BY: Rob Bowman

Robert Torrence, a scientist in Costa Rica, is infected and
dies after being splattered by sores on a wild boar. Soon
after a convict with the same name recieves a pig's leg in
the mail. He is soon covered with sores and grabbed by a
quarantine unit for examination. Two convicts, Paul and
Steve, escape from prison; they are suspicious of the
events. The X-Files team is called in to aid in the manhunt.
They realize something is up when they see a quarantine
in effect. Scully is told by a Dr. Osborne that ten men have
died from a flu-like virus. She sees the bodies being incin-
erated. Dr. Osborne is infected as one of the sores on the
bodies bursts near him. Scully discovers the package was
sent by Pinck Pharmaceuticals. Mulder traces the escapees

to Paul's girlfriend, Elizabeth, who is already infected. They find Steve dead and Paul gone. Meanwhile, Osborne admits to working for Pinck, which found a species of bug that spreads a fatal parasite. Mulder wants to warn the public but the Cigarette-Smoking Man won't allow it. Scully finds Osborne dead and is told no one will corroborate her story. Mulder boards a bus heading to Toronto with Paul on it. Paul notices him and takes a boy hostage. Paul is shot by a marksman and the quarantine unit whisks him away. Scully assures Mulder they can't go public with the experiment because they lack proof. Skinner warns them to watch their backs.

Soft Light

AIR DATE: May 5, 1995

WRITTEN BY: Vince Gilligan

DIRECTED BY: James Contner

Scully gives a student of hers, Kelly Ryan, a hand investigating a series of seeming abductions. Mulder notices an odd smudge left on the carpet of each crime scene. Finding a train ticket at a victim's house, police are led to a train station. There they encounter Dr. Chester Banton. He warns them to stay away. Upon touching his shadow they are vapourized. Mulder tracks Banton to Polarity Magnetics where he is told by Dr. Davey that Banton has been missing since an experiment in dark matter went awry. They spot Banton at the train station. Mulder cuts the lights and they apprehend him. Banton tells the agents that his shadow is like a black hole, vapourising anything it touches. He fears the government is after him to learn what he knows. Mulder asks X for help but is refused. Later, however, X and two other men show up to transfer Banton. While strapping him down, lights flicker on and the two men are vapourized. X allows Banton to escape. Banton returns to Polarity seeking Davey's help to destroy the thing. Ryan attempts to stop him and Banton sucks her into his shadow. Banton realizes Davey is a conspirator and is locked in the particle accelerator chamber. Davey alerts his bosses that he has Banton. Davey is shot; X's face is seen through the portal. The agents are shown a bogus video of Banton disappearing in the particle accelerator. Later X is told by a scientist that they will "be studying this man for a long time." Banton is shown strapped down, hooked to electrodes and looking crazy.

Our Town

AIR DATE: May 12, 1995

WRITTEN BY: Frank Spotnitz

DIRECTED BY: Rob Bowman

Mulder is intrigued by a case involving the disappearance of a federal inspector, George Kearns, who was about to close the Chaco Chicken plant. A woman at the plant, Paula, becomes delusional and is shot after she takes the manager hostage. An autopsy reveals she was forty-seven years old, but she looked much younger. She also suffered from the same rare disease that Kearns had. Dragging the river, they discover nine headless skeletons. The bones show signs of boiling, suggesting cannibalism. Kearns' wife calls the agents out of fear of Mr. Chaco, the plant founder. While she is on the phone a man in a tribal mask appears behind her. Mulder visits Chaco's house where he discovers a display case filled with human heads. Scully is bound and gagged by Chaco who takes her to a ritual attended by many townsfolk. Chaco is beheaded after an argument with the plant manager and the executioner prepares to do the same to Scully. Mulder comes to her rescue, shooting the executioner. Chaco Chicken is closed and twenty-seven people become fatally ill with Kearns' disease. Chaco's remains are never found but a worker discovers a lock of grey hair in the chicken feed while the chickens peck away at it.

Anasazi
(part 1 of 3)

AIR DATE: May 19, 1995

WRITTEN BY: Chris Carter

STORY BY: David Duchovny and Chris Carter

DIRECTED BY: R.W. Goodwin

A young Navajo man discovers a large metallic container in the desert along with an inhuman corpse. Meanwhile a computer hacker known as "The Thinker" penetrates a top secret computer system spawning calls around the globe. When the Cigarette-Smoking Man receives the call he says, "Gentlemen, that is the phone call I never wanted to get." The Lone Gunmen contact Mulder telling him The Thinker wants to meet with him to give him the stolen documents, which detail the Defence Department's UFO files. Upon receiving the files he realizes they are coded in Navajo. Scully is worried because Mulder has been acting erratic lately. In a fit he punches Skinner. Scully is told they are both in danger of losing their jobs. The Cigarette-Smoking Man pays a visit to Mulder's father to discuss the missing files. Mulder then goes to see his father, who is shot by Krycek before he can tell Mulder of his work. Scully is shot at but missed while visiting Mulder's apartment. She phones Mulder, telling him he looks guilty of his father's death due to his recent behavior. Mulder goes to Scully's where he collapses. On awakening he finds both Scully and his gun missing. Scully discovers the water in

Mulder's apartment has been drugged, which explains his recent fits. Meanwhile, Mulder sees Krycek and attacks him. He is about to kill Krycek when Scully intervenes. She shoots Mulder in the sholder to bring him down. She then takes him to New Mexico to recover. There he meets Albert Hosteen, a Navajo elder. Scully tells Mulder to find out what is in the files because her name is a recent entry. Mulder is led to the boxcar container in the desert. In it he finds what appears to be alien bodies. He calls Scully wondering "What have they done?" Suddenly the Cigarette-Smoking Man shows up in a helicopter with troops. They set the container on fire with Mulder in it and fly away. *To be continued . . .*

EPISODE SYNOPSES

SEASON THREE

The Blessing Way
(part 2 of 3)

AIR DATE: September 22, 1995

WRITTEN BY: Chris Carter

DIRECTED BY: R.W. Goodwin

The Cigarette-Smoking Man along with his troops burst into the home of Albert Hosteen demanding he tell them where Mulder is. Scully arrives later and is taken to the smouldering boxcar in the desert; she does not find any sign of Mulder. Driving away, she is stopped by a military helicopter and troops take her printed copy of the files. Scully is suspended from work for "direct disobedience." After a confrontation with Skinner she goes to Mulder's desk where she discovers the digital tape is missing. The Cigarette-Smoking Man meets with his cabal telling them things are under control. Meanwhile, Hosteen and friends find Mulder in the desert, near death. They perform a healing ritual on him. Scully, while leaving FBI headquarters, discovers a computer chip implanted in her neck. She cuts a hypnotherapy session short, afraid of remembering how the chip was implanted. At Mr. Mulder's funeral she meets the Well-Manicured Man, a member of the Cigarette-Smoking Man's cabal. He warns her she will be killed either at home or by someone she trusts. Mulder returns to his parents' house. Scully's sister Melissa calls her at home and decides to come over. Scully, paranoid about the warning, calls back to tell her to wait, but there is no answer. She leaves for Melissa's but meets Skinner who demands she get in his car. Not trusting him, they go to Mulder's apartment where Scully pulls her gun on her superior. Meanwhile Melissa is mistakenly gunned down at Scully's apartment by Krycek and another man. Skinner tells Scully he has the digital tape. Just then footsteps are heard approaching the door, distracting Scully, and giving Skinner enough time to draw his weapon, resulting in a standoff. *To be continued . . .*

Paper Clip
(part 3 of 3)

AIR DATE: September 29, 1995

WRITTEN BY: Chris Carter

DIRECTED BY: Rob Bowman

With Scully and Skinner deadlocked at gunpoint, Mulder enters his apartment, shocking the two who thought he was dead. The X-Files team force Skinner to put down his weapon. Skinner insists he hold on to the tape and reminds them that it's the only leverage they've got against the cabal. The agents take a photo of a group of men, including Mulder's father, to the Lone Gunmen. They direct the agents to a man in the photo named Victor Klemper, an amnestied Nazi scientist. Frohike enters and tells Scully of her sister's condition. The Cigarette-Smoking Man assures his colleagues that Mulder is dead and everything is under control but the Well-Manicured Man demands the tape. Klemper directs the agents to an abandoned mine in West Virginia; he then calls and informs the Well-Manicured Man. Skinner tells the Cigarette-Smoking Man he may have the tape but the Cigarette-Smoking Man tells him angrily he "doesn't make deals." At the mine Mulder and

Scully find a labyrinth of files detailing medical records of millions of people. Scully and Samantha Mulder both have files there. Mulder discovers Samantha's file was originally his own; her name was pasted over his. The lights go out, Mulder sees a craft hovering overhead, and strange beings rush past Scully. A hit squad arrives but the agents escape through a back door. Skinner meets them and tells them he wants to trade the tape for their lives. Stopping at the hospital to visit Scully's mother, Skinner is beaten up by Krycek and two other men. They steal the tape. Krycek later jumps from his car seconds before it explodes. Mulder and Scully return to see Klemper but instead find the Well-Manicured Man. He tells them of alien-human genetic experiments. Krycek calls the Cigarette-Smoking Man warning him not to make any more attempts on his life since he possesses the tape. Mulder asks his mother if she was made to choose between him and his sister. She breaks down and tells him it was his father's choice. Skinner meets with the Cigarette-Smoking Man who calls his bluff knowing Skinner doesn't have the tape. Skinner outsmarts him though, as he had Hosteen memorize the files and teach them to twenty other men. Scully's sister Melissa dies and the agents pledge to search for answers.

D.P.O.

AIR DATE: October 6, 1995

WRITTEN BY: Howard Gordon

DIRECTED BY: Kim Manners

Mulder and Scully investigate after a teenager dies when his heart is "cooked in his chest" after leaving an arcade. The agents are intrigued by the fact that five people have been struck by lightning in a rural Oklahoma town. A teenage resident of the town, Darren Peter Oswald, has recently survived a lightning strike and now possesses telekinetic powers and can summon lightning strikes. Oswald targets the husband of a woman he has a crush on, Sharon Kiveat. He jams the traffic lights at an intersection causing the husband to crash. He goes to Sharon so that they can be together but she is afraid of him. Meanwhile Mulder and Scully question Darren's friend and pinpoint Darren as the prime suspect. Mulder tries to protect Sharon but she runs away with Darren so that he won't kill them all with his powers. Mulder chases them and a confrontation ensues. Darren summons up the powers of nature when Sharon tells him she can't be with him. He fries the town sheriff and is finally apprehended by the agents. He is institutionalized and held in a high voltage room.

Clyde Bruckman's Final Repose

AIR DATE: October 13, 1995

WRITTEN BY: Darin Morgan

DIRECTED BY: David Nutter

The X-Files agents track a serial killer preying on fortune tellers. The police call in The Stupendous Yappi, a TV psychic. He calls Mulder a non-believer and asks him to leave the room. Mulder and Scully talk to Clyde Bruckman, the man who found the latest victim. They discover he can foresee people's deaths. He is reluctant to help their investigation since he can't identify the killer; he does, however, lead them to more bodies. Scully is suspicious of Bruckman, believing he may be involved. Mulder believes him to be a true psychic. Bruckman envisions a scene in which the killer murders Mulder. The killer makes it known he is targeting Bruckman so the agents hide him in a hotel room. The killer, dressed as a bell boy, enters and kills the detective watching Bruckman. But before he can kill Bruckman, Mulder chases him away. Mulder and Scully re-enact the scene Bruckman envisioned when speaking of Mulder's murder, but before the killer can strike, Scully fatally shoots him. Back at Bruckman's apartment the agents find that Bruckman has committed suicide, no longer able to deal with his "gift."

The List

AIR DATE: October 20, 1995

WRITTEN BY: Chris Carter

DIRECTED BY: Chris Carter

A death row prison inmate, Neech Manley, vows to return from the grave and kill his enemies after his execution. Only a fellow inmate knows who is on his list of five names. Mulder and Scully are called in when a guard turns up dead a few days after Manley makes his vow. The warden thinks inmates following Manley's wishes are to blame. A guard, Parmelly, tells Scully to question Roque, an inmate. Soon the head of another guard turns up in a sealed paint can. His body is later found in the warden's office. Mulder wonders if Neech Manley really has returned, while Scully believes the deaths to be the work of inmates and guards. The agents find Manley's executioner dead and his body maggot-riddled. They then question Manley's ex-lawyer. After they leave a fly buzzes around the lawyer just before he is suffocated by Neech Manley. They question Manley's wife, who seems terrified. Later they learn she is now living with the guard Parmelly. Parmelly becomes the prime suspect. Mulder and Scully, with back-ups, raid their house but find the woman fatally shot Parmelly after seeing Neech Manley in the house. The agents depart still pondering the possibilities of reincarnation. As the warden's car passes them we see a fly buzzing around him. Neech Manley appears in the backseat, sending the car into a tree at full speed and killing the warden, thereby completing the list.

2Shy

AIR DATE: November 3, 1995

WRITTEN BY: Jeffery Vlaming

DIRECTED BY: David Nutter

Mulder and Scully investigate the death of a woman found partially digested and covered in a gelatinous fluid. The case resembles a number of recent missing persons cases all involving overweight women with internet access. It appears the killer is meeting his victims on-line. Scully is hassled by a sexist detective, Detective Cross, who resents her being assigned to the case. As she prepares for an autopsy of a recent victim she is shocked to discover the body has melted into an oozing liquid. She deduces the mucous which covered the body is a digestive liquid, used by the killer to eat the woman's fat. Soon the killer, Virgil Incanto, attacks and kills a pudgy prostitute after another internet meeting scheme falls apart. The agents track down the date as a woman named Ellen. Once there, Scully gives medical aid to Ellen, who has fallen victim to Incanto. Incanto attacks Scully but Ellen rouses, grabs Scully's gun, and, with an icy stare, shoots her attacker.

The Walk

AIR DATE: November 10, 1995

WRITTEN BY: John Shiban

DIRECTED BY: Rob Bowman

Several patients at a veteran's hospital attempt suicide after their families are killed. Mulder is intrigued by a "phantom soldier," who the last suicidal patient says is preventing him from dying. A quadruple amputee patient, Rappo, tells his attendant, Roach, not to worry over the FBI's presence. The agents talk to General Callahan, the commanding officer, but he is uncooperative. Scully thinks he is covering up the insanity of his men. When they leave, Callahan sees a "phantom soldier" before his answering machine starts acting strangely. Later his aid, Captain Draper, is attacked and drowned in the pool by an unseen force. General Callahan's son sees an intruder in their house and alerts his mother. The agents arrest Roach after finding his prints in the house. He blames Rappo but the agents find Rappo is an unlikely suspect due to his disability. While under guard, the General's son is killed by the same unseen force. Mulder begins to suspect that Rappo is capable of astral projection and is seeking revenge on his superior officers from the Gulf War. The General's wife is also killed and the General is prevented from taking his own life. He goes to the hospital where Rappo traps him in the basement. Mulder bursts in and is attacked by Rappo's spirit. Meanwhile, the first suicidal veteran sneaks into Rappo's room and suffocates the sleeping man, ending the basement fight.

Oubliette

AIR DATE: November 17, 1995

WRITTEN BY: Charles Grant Craig

DIRECTED BY: Kim Manners

The X-Files team investigate the abduction of a young girl, Amy Jacobs. At the exact time she was abducted another woman, Lucy, collapses at work bleeding the victim's blood and reciting the kidnapper's words. Mulder believes there is a psychic link between the two, stemming from the fact that Lucy was abducted by the same man several years ago. Mulder asks Lucy to help him find Amy but she is reluctant, having just begun to put her life back together. Scully, along with police, suspect Lucy is somehow involved in the kidnapping. When they go to arrest her, Lucy runs away. The agents track the kidnapper to a forest hideout. When they arrive, however, they find only Lucy hiding in the basement cell. This seems to confirm Scully's suspicions but Mulder is adamant. He gets Lucy to tell him where the perpetrator is taking Amy, which is different from where the police are heading. The agents take off for a nearby river, leaving Lucy in custody with an officer. The kidnapper is attempting to drown Amy in the river; while he holds her under, Lucy begins to choke up water. Mulder finds the pair in the river and shoots the man. He performs CPR on Amy, seemingly to no avail, but she suddenly comes to as, miles away, Lucy breathes her last breath. It is determined that Lucy died as a result of drowning.

Nisei
(part 1 of 2)

AIR DATE: November 24, 1995

WRITTEN BY: Chris Carter, Howard Gordon, and Frank Spotnitz

DIRECTED BY: Rob Bowman

A video showing what is billed as an "actual alien autopsy" sends Mulder in search of a Pennsylvania crime scene. There he finds and apprehends a Japanese spy carrying satellite photos. The photos lead him to track a salvage ship which may be recovering an alien ship lost in the ocean. Meanwhile, Scully tracks down a woman whose name was in the spy's files. She finds a group of women who say they recognize the woman from her abduction. Scully also learns that they too have been abducted and had an implant removed from their necks. The implant turns out to be a chip used to track, record, and even alter her memory. Mulder meanwhile finds information about a train car. He sees what appears to be an alien being loaded into a quarantine car. X meets with Scully and warns her that the train is bound for trouble and she must make sure Mulder doesn't board it. While Scully warns him not to board, Mulder jumps onto the train. *To be continued . . .*

731
(part 2 of 2)

AIR DATE: December 1, 1995

WRITTEN BY: Frank Spotnitz

DIRECTED BY: Rob Bowman

The second instalment starts with a mass execution, Nazi-style, of a group of beings in West Virginia. Next, Scully traces her removed neck implant to a West Virginian address. In West Virginia, Scully finds frightened survivors of a leper colony. One man relates to her their ordeal involving a Dr. Yama, human experimentation, death squads, and mass graves. As he shows her the mass graves, helicopters descend, Scully is apprehended and the man shot. Mulder is busy looking for a Dr. Ishimaru on the train. He recovers the scientist's briefcase, then finds Ishimaru strangled to death. In search of the killer he goes to the quarantined boxcar where he sees the apparent alien being. Suddenly the killer attacks him; the conductor pulls a gun which Mulder gave him, saving the agent's life; attacked, he locks the killer and Mulder in the boxcar. They are trapped, without an exit code, and the killer, who is a National Safety Association agent, informs Mulder there

is a bomb on the car. Scully, in the meantime, is taken to
a friend of the Well-Manicured Man. He also tells her of
human atrocites at the leper colony before taking her to a
train car identical to Mulder's, and identical to the one she
recalls from her implant surgery. She calls Mulder and
finds out his plight. Together they locate the bomb, but
Mulder sees he has less than two hours. He believes that
someone will save him because of the important alien
cargo; Scully tells him the cargo is a human experiment
subject, and if the train blows up it will spread a deadly
disease. With only minutes to spare the agents discover the
exit code; as Mulder opens the door he is blindsided and
beaten by the NSA agent. He leaves Mulder and exits the
train car, where he is shot by X. X rescues Mulder with
seconds to spare, and the train explodes behind them. Back
in Washington, Mulder discovers that someone has
switched the briefcase he recovered from Dr. Ishimaru.
Finally, we see the Cigarette-Smoking Man watching a
Japanese translator working on the documents from Dr.
Ishimaru's briefcase.

Revelations

AIR DATE: December 15, 1995

WRITTEN BY: Kim Newton

DIRECTED BY: David Nutter

Mulder and Scully investigate the murder of an evangelist
who faked the wounds of Christ. He is the eleventh victim
murdered by a stalker whose hands burn the victim's flesh
as he strangles them. The agents are alerted to a young boy,
Kevin, who is a true stigmatic. They talk to the boy's father
who is in a mental hospital from trying to protect the boy.
Kevin is taken by his old gardener, Owen. The agents track
down and arrest Owen but Kevin escapes. Owen tells them

he is only protecting Kevin; then he jumps from a third-floor window, breaks his handcuffs, and runs off in search of the boy. Kevin, meanwhile, returns home. The killer arrives, stalking him. As he is about to kill the boy, Owen bursts in saving Kevin, but gets killed himself. Scully finds Kevin who asks her if she is the one sent to protect him. Mulder thinks it's just a case of "fanatics behaving fanatically, using religion as an excuse," but Scully's religious convictions force her to look at a more irrational explanation. Kevin and his mother are confronted by the killer, who turns out to be a rich southern businessman possibly believing he is Satan. They escape but crash their car, killing the mother. Scully vows to protect Kevin. The agents take Kevin to their hotel but the killer snatches him from their washroom. Scully tracks them to a recycling plant. She confronts the killer who jumps with Kevin into a paper shredder. The killer dies but Kevin is safe, spared miraculously from the shredder. As Kevin prepares to return to a children's shelter, Scully sees his stigmata wounds have healed. He tells her that she will see him again.

War of the Coprophages

AIR DATE: January 5, 1996

WRITTEN BY: Darin Morgan

DIRECTED BY: Kim Manners

While his apartment is being fumigated, Mulder journeys to Miller's Grove, Massachusetts, to check out recent reports of UFO activity. He finds the small town besieged by cockroaches. Three people have died — severe cockroach infestation is the only link among them. Mulder meets a pretty entomologist named Dr. Bambi Berenbaum and has what could be called a relationship with her. Together they work to solve the cockroach problem.

Meanwhile, Scully finds a fuel researcher with a licence to import dung. She thinks maybe this exotic dung has something to do with the infestation of cockroaches in the town. Mulder, on the other hand, finds evidence to suggest that the roaches are caused by an alien presence. He hypothesizes that aliens in the form of roaches have landed and our own earthly roaches are battling them for turf, resulting in heightened activity. He finds the roaches have a metallic exoskeleton. These robotic roaches are being produced by a Dr. Ivanov. Scully comes to the town to help and is caught up in a fleeing mob. She meets up with Mulder and, in an accident, the two of them wind up covered with the imported dung.

Syzygy

AIR DATE: January 26, 1996

WRITTEN BY: Chris Carter

DIRECTED BY: Kim Manners

The X-Files team answer a local detective's call for help when several small-town teens are found dead, and rumours of a Satanic cult abound. While Mulder and Scully bicker, Mulder flirts heavily with the detective, Angela White. Attending the funeral of the latest victim, the agents witness the coffin burst into flames while two teenage girls, Margi and Terri, who were with him before he died, look on holding hands. Scully thinks it's a matter for the police, not the FBI. An astrologer tells them a planetary alignment is occurring that will focus incredible cosmic energy on the town. A local mob gathers, headed by the school principal, to look for mass graves mentioned by Margi and Terri in their stories. To celebrate their birthdays the two girls kill another girl whose boyfriend they are interested in. Mulder, drinking vodka and Tang, is visited by Detective White who jumps him, pinning him to the bed, and asks him to help her "solve the mystery of the horny beast." Scully interrupts with news of the latest death. The girls meanwhile make advances on the now-dead girl's boyfriend. They wind up fighting over him, and killing him accidentally. Each implicates the other to a separated Mulder and Scully, and then the agents bring them both in for questioning. Upon seeing each other in the police station, the girls square off, objects fly around the room, and guns fire on their own. The agents wrestle the girls into a storage room and lock the door. As midnight passes the girls seemingly return to normal. The mob bursts in demanding to see them and proclaim that "it was Satan."

Grotesque

AIR DATE: Febuary 2, 1996

WRITTEN BY: Howard Gordon

DIRECTED BY: Kim Manners

A serial killer, Mostow, who paints and sculpts gargoyles, is arrested after an exhaustive, three-year search. However, the murders continue even after Mostow is incarcerated. Mulder and Scully are asked to investigate, helping Mulder's former mentor, Bill Patterson, who has a rocky relationship with Mulder. At Mostow's studio Mulder finds a secret room containing numerous corpses covered with clay and sculpted into gargoyles. Scully suspects a copy-cat killer but Mulder thinks there may be something to Mostow's belief that he was possessed. Mulder immerses himself in the case to the extent that he begins to act strangely. He is attacked by something "not human" while working late in Mostow's studio. Scully discovers Patterson requested Mulder not to test him, but because he knows Mulder will solve the case. Corpses continue to pile up while Mulder visits a terrified Mostow in prison. Returning to the studio, Mulder finds a new corpse sculpted into a gargoyle. It is agent Nemhauser, Patterson's aide. Patterson enters with clay on his hands and Mulder exposes him as the new killer. It seems Patterson had spent three long years trying to get inside Mostow's head, and now is unable to let go. He runs but Mulder apprehends him. The final scene is of Patterson behind bars screaming that he "didn't kill those people."

Piper Maru
(part 1 of 2)

AIR DATE: February 9, 1996

WRITTEN BY: Frank Spotnitz and Chris Carter

DIRECTED BY: Rob Bowman

The Piper Maru, a French salvage ship, recovers the remains of a WW II squadron. The sailor sent down to find it sees a man left alive in the sunken vessel, but an oily substance moves across his eyes and contact is lost between the Piper Maru and the diver, Gauthier. Gauthier is recovered but the suit he was wearing is covered with an oily film. Mulder and Scully are alerted when the crew of the ship are admitted to hospital in San Francisco suffering from radiation burns. Only Gauthier is unharmed. Skinner, meanwhile, is ordered to close the investigation of Melissa Scully's murder. Gauthier, on returning home, grabs his wife, and the oily substance moves across his eyes. Mulder finds him disoriented on the floor with no recollection of the events since the Piper Maru. His wife, now with the oil in her, is leaving for Hong Kong, and Mulder follows. At the airport he finds Krycek who is now selling government secrets culled from the tape he stole in *Paperclip*. Mulder, after the tape, brings Krycek back to the U.S. In the airport, however, Mrs. Gauthier corners him in the washroom and the oil goes to him. Back in Washington, Skinner is shot by a seemingly random act of violence, perhaps as a way of closing the Melissa Scully murder investigation. *To be continued . . .*

Apocrypha
(part 2 of 2)

AIR DATE: February 16, 1996

WRITTEN BY: Frank Spotnitz and Chris Carter

DIRECTED BY: Kim Manners

While Skinner is being taken from surgery, he whispers to Scully he knew the man who shot him. Scully discovers Skinner's gunman is the same one who shot her sister. Mulder brings Krycek, who now contains the alien oil, into the States. They are run off the road by agents working for the Cigarette-Smoking Man. Mulder, unconscious, doesn't see Krycek kill the agents by emitting powerful radiation. Mulder discovers Krycek's tape is missing from the locker it was in but finds in its place the phone number for the Well-Manicured Man. Scully saves Skinner's life from his would-be assassin, Luis Cardinal. Mulder finds that the Piper Maru's salvaged cargo is being stored in an abandoned missile silo in North Dakota. There the agents find more soldiers burnt to death by radiation and link them to Krycek. They pursue Krycek through the labyrinth of halls in the silo, but are stopped and forced to leave by soldiers working for the Cigarette-Smoking Man. Krycek, locked behind silo door number 13, is shown with the alien oil pouring out his eyes and mouth as it soaks into its craft. The final shot is of Krycek, pounding on the locked door and begging to be released.

Pusher

AIR DATE: February 23, 1996

WRITTEN BY: Vince Gilligan

DIRECTED BY: Rob Bowman

A man confesses to fourteen murders made to look like suicide. While being transferred in custody he hypnotizes a young deputy causing him to drive into an oncoming transport truck. Mulder and Scully are asked to help bring the killer in. Mulder thinks the man, Robert Modell, also known as the Pusher, is using mind control on people. Modell walks into FBI headquarters using mind control; he steals Mulder's file and causes a mild mannered woman to attack Skinner. The agents track him to a hospital where they discover he has a brain tumor. Mulder theorizes over the idea that brain tumors have often been linked to tele-kinesis and other paranormal senses. While detectives are staking out Modell's apartment, Modell calls and induces a heart attack on one of them. Mulder finally meets with the Pusher who controls him into playing Russian Rou-lette. As Mulder is about to shoot Scully, she runs and sets off a fire alarm. Mulder turns and fires at Modell, critically injuring him. The agents discover Modell was not seeking a cure for his tumor, rather he was using it, and the power it resulted in, to feel "like a big man."

Teso Dos Bichos

AIR DATE: March 18, 1996

WRITTEN BY: John Shiban

DIRECTED BY: Kim Manners

When people involved in the excavation and display of an ancient South American holy person's remains begin to die in a bloody, unexplained way, Mulder and Scully are called to investigate. They are told of an ancient curse connected with the shaman's remains, but Scully wonders if it's not merely a case of political terrorism. She suspects a reclusive member of the original excavation team, Dr. Bilac, who opposed the removal of the bones and has become something of a madman. While on his trail, two more museum executives meet a bloody end as if mauled by a large cat. Investigating at the museum Mulder notices all the toilets are plugged with rats. "It's as if the rats were trying to escape something," he tells Scully. They follow strange noises into a labyrinth of old steam tunnels which have long been out of use. Scully pursues the noises and discovers hundreds of stray-cats turned bloodthirsty. The cats move to attack her but she manages to escape out a steam vent. The museum is forced to hand back the artifact to the natives who return it to its burial site. The horde of cats is never found in the steam tunnels.

Hell Money

AIR DATE: March 29, 1996

WRITTEN BY: Jeff Vlaming

DIRECTED BY: Tucker Gates

The X-Files tandem investigate the death of a Chinese immigrant, cremated alive. The suspects are a group of mysterious, masked killers. Their search is aided by Detective Chao, a Chinese-American who can help them question the close-kint Chinatown community. In her autopsy, Scully discovers that a number of organs were removed from the body prior to death, causing suspicion as to a black-market organ transplant operation. They meet an old Chinese man, Hsin, whose daughter, Kim, is fatally ill. It is obvious Hsin doesn't have the money for the operation she requires. Hsin is uncooperative with the agents but

Mulder sees Detective Chao having a secretive discussion with him. Tailing Chao, the agents are led to a concealed building where a grotesque lottery is taking place. The participants risk donating vital organs against the possibility of wealth. It seems Detective Chao has been bribed into covering it up. He bursts into the room, disrupting the game, and discovers the participants have no chance of winning. A near riot ensues. Meanwhile, Mulder and Scully arrest the surgeon behind it all but he seems unconcerned. The now-wanted Detective Chao goes missing. The final scene is of Chao awakening in a crematorium about to be burned alive.

Jose Chung's "From Outer Space"

AIR DATE: April 12, 1996

WRITTEN BY: Darin Morgan

DIRECTED BY: Rob Bowman

Scully recounts a case of alien abduction to science fiction writer Jose Chung for a book in the works. The case involved two teenagers who claim alien abduction is behind their disappearance. The victims and the witnesses all have different stories which grow increasingly dissimilar and confusing; the truth is muddied. Hypnosis seems to suggest a double abduction involving two different alien beings. While performing an autopsy on the body of a supposed alien, Scully discovers it is merely a U.S. air force pilot in an alien costume. The agents wonder if the military has been abducting people for tests in the guise of aliens. Perhaps while abducting the teens, the military personnel themselves were abducted by real aliens. Or perhaps it is all a military strategy to discredit alien abduction theorists. Mysterious men in black keep appearing, warning people off the trail of aliens. Mulder questions a restauranteur about aliens while eating an entire sweet-potato pie, piece by piece. This most bizarre and comic episode continues to subvert "the truth." Only the teens themselves know if they were really abducted or if it's a cover-up for a more romantic reason. Whatever the case, Jose Chung will retell it all in his book.

Avatar

AIR DATE: April 26, 1996

WRITTEN BY: Howard Gordon and David Duchovny

DIRECTED BY: James Charleston

Mulder and Scully come to the aid of Skinner when he wakes up to find himself in bed with a dead prostitute. Skinner recalls nothing of the previous night and is uncooperative in the investigation. The X-Files team make it their misson to get to the bottom of things and clear their boss's name. They find Skinner's marriage of seventeen years is breaking up and that he is being treated by a psychiatrist for a sleep disorder that could be responsible for erratic, even violent, behavior. It seems as though their attempt to clear Skinner is backfiring and piling up evidence against him. Skinner's guilt looks even worse when his wife, Sharon, is nearly killed after being run off the road and Skinner is the prime suspect. Skinner confesses to Mulder that he doesn't know what's going on, but that he's been suffering from nightmares recently involving a ghostly old woman who terrifies him. Mulder suspects Skinner is being visited by a mythic apparition known as a succubus. The agents continue to dig and begin to uncover what appears to be a conspiracy aimed at getting rid of their boss, a conspiracy initiated by the FBI bigwigs — the

same men who had Skinner shot, and who lurk behind the
smoke of the Cigarette-Smoking Man.

Quagmire

AIR DATE: May 3, 1996

WRITTEN BY: Kim Newton

DIRECTED BY: Kim Manners

The agents investigate a series of deaths on a small lake in
Georgia famous for its resident monster, a creature similar
to the Loch-Ness Monster known as Big Blue. As people
continue to die in the lake, Mulder presses to have it closed
but Scully and the sheriff resist. While dragging the lake,
however, the sheriff is attacked by a creature, so he immediately closes the lake. Venturing out at night in a boat,
Mulder and Scully wind up stranded on a rock in the
middle of the lake. They spend a tense night involving fear,
confessions, and relationships before realizing they are
only a few feet from shore. An environmentalist tells them
the frog population in the area is dwindling rapidly. Mulder
hypothesizes that the creature, finding its frog diet lacking,
has moved on to humans for its sustenance. The environmentalist is suddenly attacked and bitten; Mulder pursues
the creature into the woods. He too is attacked but manages to shoot and kill his attacker; it turns out to be an
alligator. Mulder is dissappointed about the unlikelihood
of the lake-dwelling creature but as he looks away, we see
Big Blue emerge from the lake.

Wetwired

AIR DATE: May 10, 1996

WRITTEN BY: Matt Beck

DIRECTED BY: Rob Bowman

Quagmire

When seemingly stable people begin murdering in delusional rages, the X-Files team are alerted to the case. Scully
discovers that all the murderers watched, and recorded, a
great deal of television, and she thinks this might be a link.
Mulder notices a cable repairman acting strangely at the
scene of a recent crime, but he escapes when Mulder
pursues him. Mulder, however, discovers an odd transistor
installed in the people's cable box. Scully, after watching
hours of the murderers' tapes, also becomes delusional,
seeing Mulder meeting with the Cigarette-Smoking Man.
She fires on her partner, causing Skinner to issue a search
for her; she is now considered armed and dangerous.
Mulder takes the transistor to the Lone Gunmen who find
it is responsible for subliminal messages. It seems someone
is performing some kind of experiment. Mulder follows
the cable repairman to a large mansion where he hears
shots and finds the repairman and another man executed.
He tracks Scully to her mother's house. She again pulls her
gun on him. Eventually she relaxes and is able to forget
the subliminal messages. Mulder meets with a new ally/
source who says he is disappointed in Mulder's work on
the case.

Talitha Cumi

AIR DATE: May 17, 1996

WRITTEN BY: David Duchovny and Chris Carter

DIRECTED BY: R.W. Goodwin

Mulder begins an intensive search for a miracle healer after
a man heals numerous shooting victims with his bare
hands, then disappears in front of police. The Cigarette-
Smoking Man is also searching for this mysterious
"Jeremiah Smith." The alien bounty hunter from *Colony*
and *End Game* is also on the trail which hampers the search

considerably. Scully searches files looking for Jeremiah Smith, but finds there are many Jeremiah Smiths. Meanwhile, Mrs. Mulder falls ill. She had recently spoken in secret with the Cigarette-Smoking Man. Mulder goes to her bedside where she tells him of a secret hidden in an old family vacation home. There, Mulder discovers that his mother is more involved in things than she has let on. Meeting up with X, Mulder has a confrontaion and battle with him. With Mulder facing off against the alien bounty hunter, the approach of a mysterious deadline, and Scully wondering what to believe, the episode, and the season, come to a tense close. *To be continued . . .*

END OF SEASON THREE

MULDERISMS/ SCULLYISMS

Sarah Brennecke

(www.nashville.com/~subterfuge/xfiljoke.html)

MULDERISMS

"Did you really think you could call up the devil and ask him to behave?"

"You've gotta wonder about a country where even the president has to worry about drive-by shootings . . ."

"Before anyone passes judgment, I'd just like to remind you that we're in the arctic."

"Do you know how difficult it is to fake your own death? Only one man has pulled it off: Elvis."

"Sorry, nobody down here but the FBI's most unwanted."

". . . I changed it to 'Trust Everyone' — I didn't tell you?"

"There are more dignified ways to die than auto-erotic asphyxiation . . ."

"Oh, I didn't get his name, I was too busy getting my ass kicked."

"I would never lie. I willfully participated in a campaign of misinformation."

"You know, for a holy man, you've got quite a knack for pissing people off."

"That's good. I was worried that I would have to tell Skinner that our suspect was a giant bloodsucking worm."

"You never draw *my* bath!"

"What ever tape you found in the VCR, it isn't mine."

"Are you saying that the building's haunted? Because if you are, I think you've been working with me for too long Scully."

Lone Gunmen: "You look dull Mulder. Tell you what, you're welcome to come over Saturday night. We're all hoppin' on the Internet to nitpick the scientific inaccuracies of Earth2."
Mulder: "I'm doing my laundry."

"If you detect a hint of sarcasm in agent Scully's voice, it's because the FBI conducted a study . . ."

"You gotta love this place, every day's like Halloween."

Scully: "The answers are there, you just have to know where to look for them."
Mulder: "That's why they put the 'I' in FBI."

"So who did you tick off to get stuck with this detail, Scully?"

"No ho on the ro-jo."

Scully: "You're saying that time disappeared. Time can't just disappear, it's a universal invariant!"
Mulder: "Not in this zip code."

Scully: "Mulder, did you see their eyes? If I were that stoned . . ."
Mulder: "Ooh! If you were that stoned what!?"

Scully: "Mulder, take a look at this."
Mulder: "Do I have to?"

Ish: "I could smell you a mile away."
Mulder: "They told me that even though my deodorant is made for a woman, it is strong enough for a man."

SCULLYISMS

Scully: "There's something up there Mulder . . ."
Mulder: "I've been saying that for years."

"Last time you were so engrossed, it turned out you were reading the *Adult Video News*."

"Mulder, there is a logical explanation for everything, there has to be one for this."

"This thing chewed somebody's arm off! That's not exactly a defensive posture!"

"Mulder! You may not be who you are!"

"I'm not gonna ask if you just said what I think you said because I know it's what you just said."

"I put it back in that drawer with all those other videos that aren't yours."

"Are you sure it wasn't a girlie scream, Mulder?"

"Mulder, the truth is out there . . . but so are lies."

Mulder: "How was the wedding?"
Scully: "You mean the part where the groom passed out or the dog bit the drummer?"

Mulder: "I arranged to have the body exhumed. You aren't squeamish about that sort of thing, are you Scully?"
Scully: "I don't know, I've never had the pleasure."

"You could have shown him a picture of a flying cheeseburger and he would have said that's what he saw."

"It's an oxygen leak; even *I* can figure out what happens if they run out of oxygen."

Mulder: "Do you believe in an after-life, Scully?"
Scully: "I'd settle for a life in this one."

Scully: "I notice you drop everything fast enough in order to help her out."
Mulder: "I was merely extending her a professional courtesy."
Scully: "Oh, is that what you were extending?"

Scully: "You've got that look on your face, Mulder."
Mulder: "What look is that?"
Scully: "The kind when you've forgotten your keys and you're trying to figure out how to get back in the house."